A Reading Guide to Descartes'
Meditations on First Philosophy

Other Works of Note from St. Augustine's Press

Emanuela Scribano

A Reading Guide to Descartes' Meditations on First Philosophy

Translated by C.C. Godfrey

ST. AUGUSTINE'S PRESS
South Bend, Indiana

Library of Congress Cataloging in Publication Data
Scribano, Maria Emanuela, 1948–
[Guida alla Lettura Della Meditazioni Metafische' di Descartes.
English]
A reading guide to Descartes' meditations on first philosophy /
Emanuela Scribano; Translated by C.C. Godfrey.
pages cm.
Includes bibliographical references and index.
ISBN 978-1-58731-690-6 (clothbound: alk. paper) 1. Descartes,
Reni, 1596–1650. Meditationes de prima philosophia. 2. First
philosophy. I. Title.
B1854.S3813 2013
194 – dc23   2013008871

ST. AUGUSTINE'S PRESS
www.staugustine.net

Table of Contents

Translation's Note

In adapting Professor Emanuela Scribano's guide I have substituted citations of Italian texts with the English equivalent where appropriate. Furthermore, whereas in the original she references the Opere filosofiche (Rome-Bari 1986, IV vols.) by page number, for all references to Descartes' works I have opted to similarly help the reader and alter the citations. Excerpts from the Meditations do not refer to a specific printed edition. Rather, citations are made using meditation number in Roman numeral and paragraph number, which for the most part allow the reader to find passages easily in either the original text or various translations. All passages from the Replies to Objections include the number of the collection of objection. I have retained her use of Adam and Tannery's Oeuvres (Paris 1964–74, XII vols.) for other source material seeing as this is standard throughout Cartesian scholarship, yet to further help the reader I have added citations to Anthony Kenny's Descartes: Philosophical Letters (University of Minnesota Press 1981). For other reference works, I have provided the English translation of title and passage. In summary, although the translations are my own, I have tried to make this as universal and accurate a venture as possible and insert it into the larger body of Cartesian literature.

C.C. Godfrey

Chapter One
The Genesis of the Work

The *Meditations on First Philosophy* is a work of metaphysics. The science that we know as metaphysics was already named the "first science" by Aristotle. It deals with those things which are fixed and exist apart from bodies.[1] That is, metaphysics is concerned with incorporeal substance. Scholasticism takes this study up in its own right, and in line with this tradition Descartes' metaphysical *Meditations* makes God and the soul its subjects. The heading of the work makes this clear: "In which the existence of God and the real distinction between the soul and the body are demonstrated." In the original Latin text, Descartes prefers to use the Aristotelian nomenclature of "first philosophy," *Meditationes de prima philosophia,* a title that was changed in the French translation to read *Méditations métaphysiques touchant la première philosophie.*

Writing to his favorite correspondent, Marin Mersenne, Descartes justifies his preference for the title *First Philosophy.* "And so I send you my manuscript of the metaphysics, to which I have not yet bestowed a title (...) I believe I could call it (...) *Meditations on First Philosophy,* for therein I not only deal with God but also the soul. Yet in general, all the first principles one can know by philosophizing in the proper order."[2] The subject of

---

1   Aristotle, *Metaphysics,* 1026a. Cf. Richard Hope, trans. (University of Michigan Press: Ann Arbor, 1952), 124: "The first science, however, is a theory of entities both independent and immovable."

2   Letter to Mersenne, 11 November 1640. Adam, Charles; Tannery, Paul, eds. *Oeuvres de Descartes, Volume III.* (Paris, 1974), 239. Henceforth this work is noted simply as *AT* followed by volume and page number. See also the letter to Mersenne dated 11 November

the *Meditations* is therefore broader than a treatment of substances separated from matter—or simply God and the soul. Essentially, the first certitude that one comes to while "philosophizing in the proper order," and to which the task of founding the entirety of the system is entrusted, is the existence of the individual self. Clearly, Descartes was in search of a title which did not mask the privileged status of the certitude of the existence of one's self, as happens in the title used for the French translation: *Metaphysical Meditations.*

1. At the Heart of the *Meditations*

Descartes' interest in metaphysics emerges very early on, born in the very same years wherein he systematically took up physics, and after a period of extensive study of mathematics. Sometime between 1628 and 1629 Descartes established himself in the Netherlands and dedicated himself to the drafting of a treatise on metaphysics, which was never finished. The year 1629 marked the beginning of his study of meteors, and in 1630 he finished the *Geometry,* the work that led him to suspend work on his metaphysical tract.

In 1630 Descartes began work on *The World,* a brief text finished in 1633 that contains his physics. In the midst of writing this he confessed to Mersenne that the knowledge of God and oneself constituted the starting point of his study. He writes, "I tell you that I would not have known to find the fundamentals of physics

1640, 235: "I have not yet given it a title, but it seems to me the most fitting would be *Renati Descartes Meditationes de prima philosophia* in that I am not speaking particularly on God and the soul, but more generally of all the first things that can be known through philosophizing." Cf. Kenny, Anthony, ed. *Descartes: Philosophical Letters* (University of Minnesota Press 1981), 83. From now on references to Kenny will read *K* followed by page number. These letters can also be found in the third volume of Cottingham *et al.,* but I think it expedient to current scholarship to include references to this timely reproduction of the material.

had I not searched for them in this direction. But, yes, it is the material that I have studied the most and herein, thanks be to God, I have reached full satisfaction."[3] He later tells Mersenne that he has not completely abandoned the idea of laying out an organic treatment of metaphysics. "I cannot say that one day I will not finish a small *Treatise on Metaphysics,* which I started in Frisia. Its principal points are proving the existence of God and our souls, when they are separated from the body, and wherefore they continue in their immortality."[4] Meanwhile, again to Mersenne, he announced that in his physics he would have to deal with "many metaphysical questions," evidently convinced of the impossibility of separating the two.

The condemnation of Galileo discouraged Descartes from publishing *The World,* for the theory of heliocentrism for which the Italian scientist was condemned was essential to Descartes' physics. Descartes' metaphysics, however, was published in the *Discours de la méthode* that came out in 1637 as a preliminary to "three essays of this method," the *Dioptrique, Météores,* and *Géométrie.* The fourth part of the *Discours de la méthode* contains the first systematic exposition of Cartesian metaphysics. Yet Descartes was unsatisfied with the treatment of metaphysics that resulted from addressing too wide an audience in the *Discours.* In a work destined for the general public, he had no intention of insisting on the uncertainty of the entirety of our knowledge regarding material things, even though it is necessary that one be convinced of this uncertainty if one wants the existence of God to be shown in all evidence.[5] So he tried once more to explain his

3   Letter to Mersenne, 15 April 1630. *AT* I, 144; Cf. *K,* 8.
4   Letter to Mersenne, 25 November 1630. *AT* I, 182; Cf. *K,* 18.
5   Letter to Father Vatier, 22 February 1638. *AT* 558–565, 560. "It is true that in what I have written of the existence of God in my treatise on method I have been too obscure... The main reason for this obscurity derives from the fact that I did not dare linger too long on the arguments of the skeptics, nor say all that is necessary in order to detach the mind from the senses. It is not possible to know well the certainty and evidence of the reasons that in my method prove

metaphysics, though now with greater freedom. In 1638 he began drafting the *Meditations,* written in Latin and thereby meant for scholars, unlike the more popular *Discourse.* The *Meditations* was released in 1640. On November 11, 1640, Descartes sent the text to Mersenne, together with the objections compiled by Dutch theologian Johan de Kater (Caturus) in the summer of 1640 at the prodding of two prominent canons of Haarlem, friends of Descartes, and his responses to these objections. He requested that these texts be circulated so as to collect the objections they stirred up, in such a way so as to be able to later publish the *Meditations* with his replies to the doubts raised by a few carefully selected readers. Mersenne took care to fulfill his task of distributing the text among scholars. He gathered a series of observations that, accompanied by Descartes' responses, were added to the first printed edition of the Latin *Meditations* that came out in Paris at the end of August in 1641.[6] There are six sets of objections in the first edition: 1) one provided by Caterus, 2) a group of "various theologians and philosophers," though actually mostly by Mersenne, 3) Thomas Hobbes, 4) Antoine Arnauld, 5) Pierre Gassendi, 6) and a group of theologians, philosophers and scientists, though in reality these, too, were by Mersenne. The Cartesian responses here are critical for a comprehension of the *Meditations,* as well as for the comprehension of the evolution that Descartes' thought had to undertake in order to adequately respond to the objections placed before him. In the second edition, which appeared in Amsterdam in 1642,[7] there was included a

the existence of God well if one does not distinctly remember the uncertainty that is found in all our knowledge of material things. It does not seem fitting to include these thoughts in a book that I wish to be accessible even to the minds of women, and wherein even the most simple of minds might find enough material to take hold of its attention." Cf. *K,* 46.

6   Renati Descartes, *Meditationes de prima philosophia, in qua Dei existentia et animae immortalitas demonstrantur.* Apud Michaelem Soly, via Iacobea, sub signo Phoenicis, Parisiis 1641.

7   Renati Descartes, *Meditationes de prima philosophia, in quibus Dei*

seventh series of objections (by the hand of the Jesuit Pierre Bourdin) and Descartes' reply. There was a passage added at the end of the fourth set of objections regarding the mystery of the Eucharist, which had been left out of the first edition at the suggestion of Mersenne. Also in the second edition is a letter written to Father Dinet wherein Descartes reconstructs the genesis of the opposition to his philosophy on the Catholic front, which was mostly represented by Bourdin. On the Calvinist front, the opposition was largely in the person of Gisbert Voët, a professor at the University of Utrecht.

Before the *Meditations* was even printed, Descartes was thinking of drafting a manual which would systematize the entirety of his philosophy and be used as a compendium in schools. This, in fact, was the idea behind *Principia philosophiae* which was released in 1644. In 1647, the French translation of the *Meditations* appeared in Paris (through the Duke of Luynes) with the series of *Objections and Replies* translated by Clerselier. Descartes reviewed and approved the translation. In that same year the French translation of *Principles of Philosophy* was also released.

A long letter written by Descartes to the translator, the abbot Claude Picot, was put at the front of the *Principles*. In this introductory letter, Descartes takes up an ancient metaphor in comparing the whole of science to a tree, where metaphysics (with respect to physics) is like the roots of the trunk. "Thus, the whole of philosophy is like a tree. The roots are metaphysics, the trunk is physics, and the branches emerging from the trunk are all the other sciences, which may be reduced to three principal ones, namely medicine, mechanics, and morals."[8] This Cartesian tree

existentia et animae humanea a corpore distinctio, demonstrantur. Apud Ludovicum Elzevirum, Amstelodami, 1642.

8   *The Principles of Philosophy* in *The Philosophical Writings of Descartes, Volume I,* John Cottingham, Robert Stoothoff and Dugald Murdoch, trans. (University of Cambridge Press: Cambridge, 1984), 197. Henceforth, references to this translation of Descartes' collected works will cite the particular title, particular

turns the Aristotelian organ of the sciences on its head, where there is if anything physics which precedes and justifies metaphysics. In the Cartesian system, metaphysics plays a fundamental role with respect to physics. To understand the essence of the Cartesian metaphysical project it is necessary that one have in mind the structure of his physics and the foundational role that, according to Descartes, metaphysics plays in relation to physics.

2. The Trunk

Descartes' physics is almost completely laid out in his small treatise *The World,* or *The Treatise on Light.* This brief text constitutes a kind of breviary of modern science. In it Descartes attempts to demonstrate that matter is wholly made up of mathematical properties: third-dimensional extension and the forms any extension might assume once they are divided and put in motion through divine intervention. All of the qualitative characteristics of bodies that are perceived through the senses—sounds, colors, and smells—according to Descartes do not have any objectivity, and this is something denied by Galileo and Hobbes, as well as the most important philosopher-scientists engaged in what is now referred to as the "Scientific Revolution." That is, these qualitative characteristics do not belong to bodies. Rather, they are mental states provoked by the changes our body experiences when confronted with external bodies. Sounds, tastes, and colors exist only in the mind of the perceiving subject who translates what in matter are only mathematical properties into the language of sensible qualities. For the essence of matter consists of its extension, and matter coincides with space, therefore it has no limits. As Descartes says quite precisely, it is undefined and not infinite. He reserves that attribute for God alone. For this same reason he does not allow for a void in nature. The void, in fact, would have to be an immaterial extension, but the essence of matter is found in its

volume, particular part or meditation where applicable, and page number.

extension. Hence, the notion of the void is contradictory, and thereby impossible.

The motion imposed on the world by God in the act of creation follows very simple laws: the law of inertia (which Descartes was the first to formulate correctly), the conservation of the amount of motion originally put in the world by God, and the tendential straight lines of movement. In analyzing the nature of bodies and the formulation of the three rules which govern motion, Descartes radically departs from an Aristotelian physics, stripping objects of their qualitative characteristics (which Aristotelian physics maintains to be truly part of the object). Nature is freed from any kind of anthropomorphism, especially from the presumed tendency of all natural motion towards rest since, based on the law of inertia, matter is in the end indifferent both to rest and motion. Descartes likewise rejects Epicurean physics, all on account of his rejection of the void.

With matter created by God and motion ordered by laws, imposed on the original matter, Descartes claims to be able to explain every physical phenomenon. *The World* presents itself as a mental experiment whose point of departure is the theory of creation of indefinitely extended matter, all divided into parts and set in motion by God. He reconstructs the genesis of the universe, showing its formation in every detail without requiring any empirical evidence as proof. Descartes' physics is a "fairy tale," yet unlike true fairy tales, at the end of this one we know how the real world is, and whether a world actually exists.

3. The Roots

In *The World*, the laws of nature are based on the nature of God. As God is unchanging, God continues to conserve the particles of matter in the same way in which he created them. Hence, all particles of matter "continue always to be in the same state so long as collision with others does not force it to change that state."[9]

---

9   *The World* in *The Philosophical Writings of Descartes, Volume II*, John Cottingham, *et al.*, 93.

Inasmuch as God is unchanging, the amount of movement originally imposed on the world remains the same, despite the passage from rest to motion in the collision of bodies. Inasmuch as God is unchanging, bodies are always conserved with the same tendential movement. Inasmuch as the tendential movement compatible with an instantaneous divine conservation of matter is straight-line motion, the principle by which bodies move according to a straight-line tendential motion holds true. One sees that a major part of Cartesian physics, in order to determine the laws of nature, is based on divine nature and the relationship God enters into with the world.[10] Knowledge of the nature of God is thereby indispensable in establishing the most telling part of the content of the science of physics. This is the first stage of the fundamental role that metaphysics plays in the development of physics. It is most likely this role that Descartes alludes to in the famous letter to Mersenne on April 15, 1630, wherein he declares to have begun studies engaging the knowledge of God, and that it would not have been possible to come to "the foundations of physics" if he had not embarked on that route.[11] It must be said that in the *Meditations* there is no trace of this foundational dimension of metaphysics compared to physics, but not because the *Meditations* does not deal outright with physics. It is quite the contrary.

It is again to Mersenne that Descartes says, "Between you and me, I must confess that these six meditations contain all the fundamentals of my physics. But I beg you not to say so, for the Aristotelians would then likely hinder their acceptance. I would hope that those who read them adjust themselves to my principles and recognize the truth in them before realizing that they destroy those of Aristotle."[12] The fundamentals of physics that Descartes speaks of in this letter are distinguished in the analysis of the

10 Analogous foundation of the laws of nature in *Principles of Philosophy*, §§ 36, 39, and 42 in *The Philosophical Writings of Descartes, Volume II*, John Cottingham, *et al.*, 77.
11 See above, note 3.
12 Letter to Mersenne, 28 January 1641. *AT* III, 297–298. Cf. *K*, 94.

nature of matter, or to be more precise in the reducing of the essences of bodies to mere mathematical properties that are above all theorized in the fifth meditation. Contrary to the laws of nature, the mathematics that describes the nature of bodies is neither derived—nor deducible—from divine nature. Nevertheless, metaphysics plays a central role with respect to these principles. Essentially, metaphysics is entrusted with the task of guaranteeing that what the mind knows as constituting the essence of matter, actually constitutes its nature. Metaphysics, which can say nothing of the nature of matter, is actually indispensable in guaranteeing the truth of the knowledge that human minds have of the world. Here, metaphysics plays an epistemological role.

Descartes is convinced that physics is properly composed entirely of "clear and distinct" ideas, or ideas that have the essence of the things which ideas represent as their objects. The clarity and distinction of an idea is verified by the effect that the presence of this idea produces in the mind: it is impossible to doubt these ideas when they are present to an attentive mind. On the contrary, all of Aristotelian science is made up of "obscure and confused" ideas whose correspondence to the reality of things the mind can always doubt. It would seem that the criterion of clarity and distinction of ideas, together with the indubitability that comes with it, might be enough to fully ensure the truth of Cartesian science. Yet Descartes maintains that this criterion is not sufficient. Faced with clear and distinct ideas, it is, in fact, always possible to question whether the certainty that comes with this clarity and distinction and one's incapacity to deny them his consent is good enough of a condition to hold them furthermore as true. The human mind is finite, hence its certainty cannot be taken up as a measure of truth. On the basis of the finite nature of the human mind and furthermore drawing upon the Christian reflection of infinite divine power, skepticism found new arguments that challenged the capacity to arrive at the truth: God, who created the mind, maintains full power over it, and could make it so the undeniable assent the mind gives to clear and distinct ideas does not actually correspond to the truth.

Descartes, for his part, does nothing to undermine the discrepancy between the human mind and God. His theory of knowledge is quite far from the intent to secure access to the truth according to the participation of the human mind in the realm of the divine (following the Augustinian suggestion, which in the 1600's garnered more favor). In fact, Descartes advances a theory of the origin of ideas, inneism, by which ideas are thought to be inscribed in the human mind and thereby it is in the mind rather than in God that true knowledge can be traced. Yet the autonomy of the human mind over the divine mind as seen in inneism did not satisfy Descartes. He took this ever further, and even claimed that the content of innate ideas was freely created by God and could have been different than what it is. As mathematical ideas are innate ideas, even the mathematics upon which physics is founded might have been different if God had so desired.

According to Descartes, mathematics deals with simple natures, such as points, lines, and numbers, all that which man has not created, but only "discovers." From these he passes on to theorems and demonstrations. Inasmuch as they are not the work of man, one must in reality search for the relationship these natures have with God, in what way they are caught up in him. The question about the relations in mathematics, and likewise of the essences of bodies to the divine nature, is a matter of ancient tradition. Descartes, as we will see more clearly later on, has a Platonic conception of mathematics that deals with essences independent both from the human mind as well as things existing in nature. Hence, he has before him two choices: the Platonic way, strictly speaking (the essence of material things is independent from the divine nature and co-eternal with God), or the way of Christianized Platonism (the essences of things are found in God and identify themselves with the nature of God). The latter was chosen by Galileo and reproduced in his theory of mathematics. And yet Descartes rejects both of these directions. With respect to Christianized Platonism, Descartes refuses to equate the essences of things with the divine nature, and confronted with pure Platonism, he refuses to accept a kind of separate divinity co-eternal with God. Rather, for Descartes the idea of God who is one and infinitely powerful, imposed on the philosophical culture by Christianity, obliges him to maintain that the essences of things have been freely created by God as has been individual existence. Descartes always presents this theory as a necessary consequence of recognizing the infinity and incomprehensibility that one must necessarily accept if one does not want to fall into Atheism.[13]

In a famous letter to Mersenne dated April 15, 1630, Descartes announces that in his treatise on physics, at the time almost complete, he would discuss some metaphysical questions and cites as an example his most original theory of metaphysics, according to which God has freely created not only existing things, as all Christian philosophy has always maintained, but also the essences of things (and this is a position contrary to what all of philosophy held as true until that moment). Inasmuch as the essences of things consist of mathematical characteristics—tri-dimensional extension and its figures—God has freely created also numbers and figures. Despite this declaration, the doctrine known as the "free creation of eternal truths" does not appear at all in *The World*. Neither does it come up in *Metaphysical Meditations* nor in later works in print. The only time it is mentioned is in his replies to the fifth and sixth objections to the *Meditations*. This latter circumstance is enough to exclude that Descartes decided to not make this doctrine public for reasons of prudence. Neither can one conclude that there was a withdrawal of the doctrine. Rather, Descartes continued to work on it for the rest of his life through the unending exchange of letter between himself and several inter-locutors, above all Antoine Arnauld, the English philosopher Henry More, and the Jesuit Pierre Mesland.

The most simple explanation of why the doctrine of the free creation of eternal truths is absent in the *Metaphysical Meditations* is that the project of giving a foundation to the truth as seen in this work does not take as its privileged interlocutor the

13   Cf. Letter to Mersenne, 6 May 1630. *AT* I, 149–150. Cf. *K,* 12.

God who could have made it so 2+2 does not equal four, rather the more traditional image of God. In other words, Descartes means to defend science from those objections, even theological, that might be made against it by theologians and philosophers who have never thought that God might have power over the essences of things, on mathematics and laws of logic, yet nonetheless has full power over the minds of man. Indeed, it is sufficient to think that God might exercise his power over finite minds—and as created by God depend on God—to doubt that human science is able to truthfully describe the world. On the whole, for theologians and modern skeptics it was enough to consider that the human mind could be host to illusion and deception to see how they would incapable of arriving at the truth. Therefore, even if 2+2 were necessarily equal to four, and not even God could have made it otherwise, God could have created in the human mind the irresistible consent to a different answer. In this case, the human mind would necessarily judge that 2+2 is equal to five, and never know that things are actually different than they appear. This is the outcome that a recognition of divine omnipotence sets in motion, and it is precisely this outcome against which human science must defend itself.

4. Descartes' Project

The main issue in the *Meditations* is somehow ensuring that human science is competent to speak in truth about the world. In order to be certain that that which appears to be true to the human mind is not merely an appearance, it is necessary that one know much concerning the way of God. This is why in Descartes metaphysics is the foundation of physics. Only the knowledge of the nature of God can answer the question of the possibility of uncorrectable fallacy of the mind.

The knowledge of God relative to this project, and hence the knowledge of God to which the *Meditations* is dedicated, is strictly limited to the function of guaranteeing the truth which God himself deposits in science. There are two attributes of God that one must know in order to accomplish this: infinite potency, by which God might cloud human knowledge, and its veracity, which would thereby guarantee that God cannot will to use his power to this end.

Descartes' project stands out in its peculiarity amidst the alternative scientific foundations of his day. The presumption of complete separation between the human and divine mind produced the conventionalism of Thomas Hobbes. According to Hobbes, one only has true knowledge of something if one knows its origin. He who *really* knows something has actually, then, produced the thing in question. Yet Hobbes claims that mathematics is human work and so entirely subject to the finite mind. The world, rather, is God's work and therefore the human being does not and cannot know the nature of it. Consequently, knowledge of the world through mathematics can never really tell us what things are, but only how or in what way the human mind knows them. Reality remains inaccessible to the finite intellect. The separation of the human mind from God allows for the construction of a sure science, though necessarily hypothetical or conjectural. This sure science is mathematical physics.

Rather, the Cartesian project claims that human knowledge might reach the essences of things and, contrary to conventionalism, rests on inneism. That is, it leans on the presence—in the mind—of ideas that are not the work of the mind itself, and on account of these it is possible to know the nature of material things.

On the other hand, inneism holds that ideas are known from within the mind itself and not through participation in the divine mind. In this way, Descartes rejects both the Conventionalism of Hobbes as well as the resurfacing Augustinianism—the latter which, in order to justify the necessity and universality of knowledge, invokes an emanation from God of an illumination that allows the mind to obtain, or attain, truth directly from its source, in God.

Yet the assurance of the truth in human science is not the only fundamental aspect of physics that metaphysics is called upon to realize. The theory of knowledge, which Descartes must undo in order to establish his science, requires a metaphysical justification, too. This time, however, it is not God that one must speak of, rather the other prized object of the metaphysical inquiry—the soul (or more specifically, the mind in its nature and in its relation to the body). According to Descartes, mathematics is not obtained through abstraction and the elaboration of the data received through sensory experience. Nor is it a construction of the mind. In order to justify this double rejection, Descartes has to construct a theory that founds the possibility of acquiring true knowledge independently of the senses and of the free activity of the mind. This theory is what we call inneism: the mind knows the essences of things through the bundle of ideas that are part of the very nature of the intellect.

Inneism is justified by Descartes through a theory of the nature of the mind and its relationship to the body. The mind and the body are two distinct substances and have different natures. This is how the mind can have knowledge independent of the senses by way of ideas that are written into one's very nature. Even here Descartes turns to the Platonic tradition, as opposed to the Aristotelians who instead maintain that the body and soul make up one single substance and used this anthropological theory to justify empiricism as well. Nevertheless, we will see that Descartes abandons Plato when he himself begins to theorize on the relation between the mind and the body.

The foundational role that metaphysics plays with regard to physics calls for an investigation or inquiry of God (to ensure the truth of knowledge) and the nature of the mind (to support inneism). The main body of the *Meditations* is dedicated to these two themes. Physics is present as something to be established through the theory of the mathematical nature of matter.

It is helpful to map out all of the theories that must be developed in order for the Cartesian initiative of founding the metaphysics of science to succeed.

a) Physical theories
   1. Matter is structured mathematically.

2. The qualitative characteristics that are perceived by the senses are merely subjective (unlike Aristotelian-Scholastic physics).

b) Gnoseological theories
1. The essences of things are known independently of experience.
2. The ideas of mathematics are innate (as opposed to the Empiricism of Aristotelian science and Conventionalism).

c) Metaphysical theories necessary for the possibility of the theories compiled in "b":
1. The mind is truly distinct from the body (contrary to the Aristotelian idea of the mind as form of the body).
2. Essence is distinct from existence (contrary to the Aristotelian position and, in general, the empiricist position regarding the priority of existence over essence).

d) Metaphysical theories necessary to establish the truth of the theories compiled in "a":
1. God exists.
2. God is not a liar.

Metaphysics, then, plays a prominent role in the foundation of physics, and this explains its extraordinary complexity and accuracy. Yet the fact remains that with respect to the content of physics it is merely an instrumental science. This explains Descartes' surprising recommendation. He who dedicated so much time to the construction of his metaphysics advises us not to waste so much time on this subject. Instead one should accept the results of the lengthy trial by Descartes and pass on to the sciences which are indeed crucial for man: above all physics, and secondly medicine. "Keep in mind that one must not exaggerate one's time spent on the meditations and metaphysics overall ... it is enough to have acquired a general knowledge of it and remember its conclusions. Otherwise the mind becomes too distracted by the physical and sensible things and thereby incapable of actually taking them into consideration, and this is the human endeavor that we must more finely cultivate.... On the other hand, the author deals sufficiently with the truth of metaphysics and has established its certitude in such a way as to allow others to forego a long and arduous reflection of these matters."[14]

No human being lives in the foundations of his house, nor does any bird make a nest in the roots of a tree. Nevertheless, it is necessary to build a solid foundation and robust roots so that the house and the nest will be stable habitats. This is what Descartes hoped to have accomplished once and for all, and for all men, in his *Meditations on First Philosophy.*

14 Descartes to Burman. *AT* V, 165.

Chapter Two
The Structure of the Work

Descartes chooses the template of a meditation to elaborate on his metaphysics. This idea was borrowed from the spiritual and religious genres of literature. This literary genre came onto the scene as the description of the path of he who searches for salvation beginning in the shadow of sin. Religious meditations are didactic pieces in which personal experience serves as a guide for readers more through examples than with doctrine, following the current or flow of events that brought the author to this salvation. Using this method, the Cartesian *Meditations* translates the search for spiritual salvation into a search for speculative salvation, or salvation of concepts. One must free himself from the errors and prejudices born of a faith carelessly attached to sensory knowledge. Likewise, one must abandon the cultivated systemization of these prejudices, as represented by Aristotelian Scholasticism. From the shadows of error and the prison that is sensible knowledge, the reader will rise and put himself on the way that leads to the light of truth.

If the reader wishes to understand he must be proactive in his approach. Since it is about running alongside the author and his experience, the reader will himself also have to meditate. The material is thereby divided into meditations and not chapters, which prescribe time spent on each in order that the route taken becomes an integral part of the intellectual life of the reader. The *Meditations* aims to convince, not conquer: "... no one can conceive something so well, and make it his own, when he learns it from someone else as when he discovers it himself."[1] This is all the

---

1   *Discourse on the Method* in *The Philosophical Writings of Descartes, Volume I,* Cottingham, *et al.,* 146.

more necessary insofar as metaphysics is a discipline that begins with propositions quite far removed from sensory experience, and thereby requires that things be slowly absorbed so as to penetrate the mind and lead it to acknowledge those principles which are obscured by the strong force of one's prejudices. "This is why I wrote 'Meditations' rather than 'Disputations,' as the philosophers have done, or 'Theorems and Problems,' as the geometers would have done. In so doing I wanted to make it clear that I would have nothing to do with anyone who was not willing to join me in meditating and giving the subject attentive consideration."[2]

Descartes is talking about an *itinerarium mentis*, which holds for both the discovery as well as the conviction. In this project of leading one to the truth by way of persuasion, we see that some demonstrations that Descartes judges to be too innovative are reformulated in a more colloquial style, assuming the teacher-student formula of Aristotelian argumentation. This happens in the second and third meditation. We will come back to these. As for the rest, in his letter to Mersenne cited above wherein he incites his interlocutor to say nothing of the *Meditations* containing his physics, Descartes writes of his persuasive technique and that he hoped "that those who read them will unconsciously become accustomed to my principles and recognize the truth in them before realizing that they actually destroy the tenets of Aristotle."

Still adhering to the logic of a meditation, one soon observes that at the beginning of this journey there are materials used which come from the same tradition that one is attempting to undermine. Insofar as this journey is driven by the desire to free oneself from prejudices, these very prejudices are all that we have when we start off. This is why only along the way are certain concepts which were used but not clearly analyzed clarified. Contrary to what occurs in a treatise, then, the very operative instruments in the meditations are subject to revision and clarification as the

2   "Replies to the Second Set of Objections," in *The Philosophical Writings of Descartes, Volume II,* Cottingham, *et al.,* 112.

work unfolds. The new human being expected to emerge from this meditative passage would no longer recognize many of these notions and reasons as his own, even though they were his at the start. As we shall see, this is particularly evident in the notion of God as introduced in the first meditation, but it holds true for the idea of mathematics as well. The fullness of clarity on this point comes only in the fifth meditation.

The fact that the element of persuasion is fundamental to the Cartesian *Meditations* must not be interpreted as a mechanism of rhetoric. The meditative process is, in fact, held to a method which is at once both demonstrative and logically correct. It is what Descartes calls "the order of reasons," or the precept according to which "the items which are put forward first must be known entirely without the aid of what comes later; and the remaining items must be arranged in such a way that their demonstration depends solely on what has gone before."[3] Internal to the act of meditating, things "proposed to be primary" are not, however, necessarily what logically establish what comes next. Rather, they are those things which have been discovered first and what in the order of discovery do not depend on what follows. The order of reasons must be respected if one desires his reasoning to be persuasive *and* logically correct, though the demonstrative route can assemble itself according to an analytic or even synthetic agenda. With the analytic agenda, the order of reasons follows the hierarchy of the discovery. The first truths are those discovered first and whose persuasiveness is not dependent on anything else. The synthetic agenda looks instead to the hierarchy of the logical foundation. The first truths are those that *in the order of logic* do not depend on, or follow from, anything else.

Descartes is convinced that in metaphysics the analytic method is more beneficial inasmuch as it is more like a discipline that has to fight against the inclinations of the senses, beginning with its first principles. Hence, in trying to convince it meets with

3   Ibid., 112. Cf. Letter to Mersenne, 24 December 1640. *AT* III, 266–70. Cf. *K, 85.*

acute difficulty. Geometry, however, can help itself to the synthetic method thanks to a greater conformity of its first principles with sensory knowledge. The straight line being the shortest line between two points seems intuitively true because it easily lends itself to an imaginative test. Metaphysics, however, deals with entities—God and the soul—which cannot be imagined, much less reached by the senses. Hence, to yield results it must work against the habit to accept as true only what is attainable by the senses and the imagination. To meditate and follow the order of what is firstly known must help one overcome the particular difficulties of metaphysics.

The style of meditating, convincing, and involving the reader in the pursuit of truth-discovery provides an initial explanation of why the text remains in the first person for the duration of the work. Even when Descartes displayed his philosophy for the first time in the *Discourse on the Method,* he did so in an autobiographical style, and once again in the first person. When he agreed to expound his metaphysics according to an impersonal geometric form, he did so either against his will to satisfy a request on the part of Mersenne (in the appendix to the *Replies to the Second Objections*) or with a more systematic intention meant to win over the institutional and academic crowd, as he does in his *Principles.* Yet when he delineates his philosophy and is free to choose his style, Descartes opts for an autobiographical tone, and a kind of narrative given in the first person. Yet there is still a difference of style between the *Discourse on the Method* and the style of the *Meditations.* The self in the *Discourse on the Method* is the object of the narration, and is therefore properly speaking an autobiography. In this work, past tense is favored. On the other hand, the self in the *Meditations* is the author of the narration. Its story develops before the very eyes of the reader. This is why here the present tense is used most consistently.

The analytic sequence and meditative template solidifies the centralization of the *Meditations* on the "I," or the self. The first truths are neither those which logically establish the argumentative route (the first principles) nor that which ontologically establishes the system itself (God). Rather, the first or preliminary truths are those which the subject, or reader, comes to first through being convinced. Nevertheless, founding metaphysics on the self is not reducible to simply a choice of method. Rather, it is *commanded* by the Cartesian metaphysical project. Again, this project is the attempt to base the truth of science in an ordering set apart from the infinite, pivoting on what one can know to be absolutely true, starting from the finite subject. The first truth that Descartes identifies in this way is that of the existence of the thinking "I," or one's self. All other truths are also obtained from within thought—including the existence of God. The self, then, is both the protagonist and center of the Cartesian system of metaphysics.

The stages of meditation are declared in each title of the *Meditations*. The first, "What Can Be Called Into Doubt," is dedicated to recognizing all opinions formed prior to undertaking the search for truth and actively placing all things in doubt. The second, "The Nature of the Human Mind, and How It Is Better Known than the Body," contains the discovery of the first indubitable premise—the existence of the self, the "I." The third, "The Existence of God," is concerned with the existence of a truthful God who safeguards the truth of indubitable ideas. The fourth, "Truth and Falsity," analyzes the origin of errors in judgment and demonstrates its compatibility with divine truthfulness. The fifth, "The Essence of Material Things, and the Existence of God Considered a Second Time," uses divine truthfulness to guarantee the knowledge the human mind has of the nature of bodies, inasmuch as their natures are made up solely of quantifiable characteristics. Here Descartes elaborates on the theory of inneism, and in light of this he once again elaborates on the existence of God. Lastly, the sixth meditation, "The Existence of Material Things, and the Real Distinction Between the Mind and Body," salvages the existence of one's own body, and external bodies, from the doubt of the first meditation on account of divine truthfulness.

Chapter Three
Analysis of the Work

1. Doubt, the Indubitable, and What Is True

The first meditation opens by declaring the intention of seeking a firm and hardy foundation in the sciences. This foundation cannot be picked out of the opinions held as true up until now. For experience often shows that the force of our prejudices imposes opinions upon us that seem absolutely true, though later they are revealed to be false. To carve out a solid base on which to build one's knowledge, it is critical that one utilize a criterion by which to discriminate among the beliefs picked up throughout the course of one's life. This criterion is the indubitability.

1.1. *Doubt as a Method*

The Cartesian project of founding science proposes to eliminate all opinions subject to doubt in search of those indubitable premises upon which it would be possible to erect a structure of science no longer up for revision. In this enterprise skepticism is, on the one hand, an enemy to be faced, and on the other hand the ally with which one gauges the grip beliefs that are accepted without scruple during our lives have on us. In the *Synopsis of the Meditations,* Descartes underlines the two-fold function of doubt. First, doubt must serve to free the mind from its prejudices. Second, doubt must eliminate the possibility of later questioning what is now discovered to be true. He says of "the usefulness of such extensive doubt" that "its greatest benefit lies in freeing us from all of our preconceived opinions (...) The eventual result of this doubt is to make it impossible for us to have any further doubts about what we subsequently discover to be true."[1] If, after placing every belief in doubt according to the praxis of skepticism, one finds that one or more beliefs are actually indubitable, one thereby finds the basis upon which to construct a science on certitude.

Cartesian doubt, then, is geared towards the search for indubitability. But the indubitability that Descartes seeks is not understood in a psychological sense, as that which one cannot be doubtful of, but in a normative sense as well. That is, as that which is not subject to even the "slightest doubt." That means that even a weak and far-fetched doubt emanating from common sense is enough to put one's certitude of something up for debate. On the other hand, this means there must always be some real, or at least plausible, reason for doubting. Two positions, then, are not allowed: being satisfied with high probability, but also doubting to an indefinite degree when there is no grounds to do so and one does so gratuitously. This is the bond and challenge that Descartes poses to skepticism: if the skeptic is to be worthy of attention, he must advance reasons that justify his doubt.

Along the trial of doubt, Descartes is not satisfied in underlining uncertainty of the whole of a category of beliefs, but because of this uncertainty demands that such individual beliefs ought to be rejected as false. Doubt is "hyperbolic" because it transforms indubitability into a judgment of falsehood. In this way doubt is an exercise used to temporarily suspend all opinions which until this moment of suspension occupied space in the mind. The Cartesian request to move doubt into full-on negation can be satisfied on account of the particular way judgment is constructed. Descartes discusses this in the fourth meditation. According to Descartes, assenting to a proposition or premise is always voluntary. The intellect limits itself to hosting ideas and the relation between ideas, while the truth-value of this relation (whether the rod submerged in water that looks split is actually split, or whether 2+2 is equal to four) is a matter of the will. There is only

---

1   "Synopsis of the Six Following Meditations," in *The Philosophical Writings of Descartes,* John Cottingham, *et al.,* 9.

one instance wherein the will necessarily intervenes—when the relation between the concepts contained within a proposition is itself necessary. For example, it is impossible to deny that two plus three equals five inasmuch as negating this relation yields a contradiction. In all other cases, the will has the power to affirm, deny, or suspend judgment. If the content of a proposition is uncertain, the will remains free and can, rather than adjust according to a suspension of a judgment of the doubtful content of the proposition, accept this content as true or reject it as false. To the person who denies the will this potency, and maintains that the most the will can do is judge to be doubtful the relations between ideas which are not necessary, Descartes can respond that the freedom of the will with respect to what is pertinent to the intellect is already demonstrated by the fact that, up until now, this same pertinent content has already been deemed true according to the prejudices of the senses even if in some way dubious. This same judgment has freely (and arbitrarily) passed over data provided by the intellect. So it is about choosing the opposite, though this is possible for the same reason it has been until now possible to judge as true that which is only probable. That is, we are talking about overcoming the arbitrary, or that by which the will assents to probable relations, with some other arbitration, that with which the will now chooses to declare probable relations as false. Cartesian doubt is the result of a free choice with respect to data offered by the intellect. "The mind uses its own freedom and supposes the non-existence of all the things about whose existence it can have even the slightest doubt."[2]

If the will adjusts to the perception of the intellect and would cease to act freely, it would never succeed in liberating itself from prejudices, for the "ancient and stock opinions" are after all probable and would enchant and enchain the intellect in the force of their likeness to the truth. "I shall never get out of the habit of confidently assenting to these opinions, so long as I suppose them to be what in fact they are, namely highly probable

2   Ibid.

opinions–opinions which, despite the fact that they are in a sense doubtful, as has just been shown, it is still much more reasonable to believe than to deny. In view of this, I think it will be a good plan to turn my will in completely the opposite direction and deceive myself, by pretending for a time that these former opinions are utterly false and imaginary."[3] Following the decision to transform all doubtful judgments into negative judgments, the mind creates a space temporarily clouded by prejudices and all prior beliefs, wherein one can undertake the project of searching for the indubitable.

The decision to render false everything whose truth contains some reason for doubt sets up the criterion for what is true by way of opposition: that which is true is that which cannot be touched by any thinkable reason of doubt. True and false are the only categories Descartes allows, both of which are discriminated by doubt. The artificial method of temporarily judging to be false every doubtful opinion shows right away the limits or boundaries of Cartesian investigation. There is no interest for probable sciences or what is likely to be true—what one is looking for is only the true science, real science.

1.2. *The Object of Doubt*

In the summary preface to the *Meditations,* Descartes makes it clear that doubt revolves mainly around material things. "In the First Meditation reasons are provided which give us possible grounds for doubt about all things, especially material things."[4] And it is, in fact, a perfect science of material things that he wants to acquire. To this end, Descartes is determined to put previously

---

3   *Meditations on First Philosophy* in *The Philosophical Writings of Descartes, Volume II,* John Cottingham, *et al.,* "First Meditation", 15.When citing particular passages from the *Meditations* that are part of the individual meditations, I will replace the title of the meditation with the Roman numeral followed by the page number that corresponds specifically to Cottingham.

4   "Synopsis of the Following Six Meditations," in *The Philosophical Writings of Descartes, Volume II,* John Cottingham, *et al.,* 9.

assumed beliefs into question, testing the consistency of the principle that stands at the head of it all, that "the truest and most sure kind of knowing" derives from the senses. The Cartesian project aims in the first place to put into question every science that, as in Aristotle, is constructed on the basis of the generalization of sensory data. Here, Descartes' intention is to dismantle these sciences. In the second place, this project aims to test the Cartesian science already structured according to the mathematical perspective of the world, and hence parting ways with the data of our senses.

According to Descartes, Aristotelian science is nothing other than an educated systematization of the spontaneous and ingenuous beliefs of common sense. To combat the Aristotelian sciences, the arguments that classical skepticism has accumulated against the certainty of sensible knowledge are sufficient, both inasmuch as this knowledge claims to attest to the existence of external bodies, as well as in it claim to provide what is needed in order to know the nature of these bodies.

Beliefs based on experience are hit with a series of waves of doubt wherein the meditative progression of the text emerges as particularly evident. The subject is cut in half, resulting in a "meditating self" and an "old self," and between these two figures there is established a driving dialogue in which the meditating self, who has decided to question all his past knowledge, submits a series of reasons to the old self, the self immersed in prejudices and resistant to let them go, of why to doubt the trustworthiness of the knowledge obtained through the senses. The old self, in turn, tries to counter the reasons to doubt that threaten his certainty, and with every victorious wave coming from the assault of the meditating self the old self tries to embed itself in an ever more withdrawn position, one which ever more individuates a level of certainty in knowledge derived from the senses.

In the first place, the meditator invokes the familiar experience of the betrayal of the senses. Sometimes our senses deceive us, so it is best to remove all faith in the knowledge one might attribute to them. "Whatever I have up till now accepted as most true I have acquired either from the senses or through the senses. But from time to time I have found that the senses deceive, and it is prudent never to trust completely those who have deceived us even once."[5] Nevertheless, replies the old self, the betrayal of the senses is limited to minute and distant things and does not have much to do with immediate and macroscopic experiences, "for example, that I am here, sitting by the fire, wearing a winter dressing-gown, holding this piece of paper in my hands."[6] Only those without their wits let themselves be betrayed by this kind of experience. But, the meditator comes back to object, saying that to place the certainty of this data in doubt it is not necessary to consider himself crazy. It is enough that he invokes a very familiar possibility— dreams. Even dreams sometimes seem to be so real and vibrant that because of these internal qualities it makes it hard to distinguish them from waking moments. Hence, not even the closest and clearest sensory experiences are capable of attesting to the existence of something outside the mind. Judgments based on experience presuppose the existence of the beings experienced outside the mind as well as the likeness of these beings to the perception of them in the human mind. The dream theory is devastating, for it allows the possibility that the whole of existence is merely a mental construction and nothing exists beyond our thought. If I dream, it is not true that "I am here, sitting next to the fire, in my dressing gown, with this paper in hand."

Nonetheless (and here comes the old self back to fight), it seems that something independent from the mind has to exist. Even if all sense experience were a dream, the prime elements of dream-like experience cannot be the fruits of fantasy. A painter can easily invent abstract or imaginary scenes, yet the paints he uses are not strictly considered a part of his art. So, if bodies do not exist outside my mind as I perceive, and if my experience is fantastical and dream-like, at least corporeal nature and its extension, the figure of extended or projected things, quantity, breadth,

5 *Meditations* in *The Philosophical Writings of Descartes, Volume II,* John Cottingham, *et al.,* I. 12.
6 Ibid., 13.

number, place, time, etc. must be "true." That is, they must be independent from the artistic project of the painter—they are the paints he uses to paint an imaginary animal. The destructive capacity of doubt based on the dream theory reaches its limit in the endurance (survival, if you will) of some primary characteristics of external bodies which, as in the dream theory, maintain their independence from the activity of the mind. Otherwise, the dream itself, like an artist's painting, would be impossible.

Not everything that I believe to be independent from the mind reveals itself to be, in the end, purely subjective. That is, so concludes the old self: within the terms of the process of analysis of empirical data I am thrown among elements that cannot be broken down further, and thereby simple, universal, and independent from the mental activity of the knowing subject. The first elements in which one can sort out sense experience are constituted by the quantitative characteristics of bodies:

> Although these general kinds of things—eyes, head, hands, and so on—could be imaginary, it must at least be admitted that certain other even simpler and more universal things are real. These are as it were the real colours from which we form all the images of things, whether true or false, that occur in our thought. This class appears to include *corporeal nature in general, and its extension; the shape of extended things; the quantity, or size and number of these things; the place in which they may exist, the time through which they may endure,* and so on.[7]

The argument surrounding dreams leaves the mathematical structure of sensible experience intact. The proof that the dream hypothesis is powerless (in this case, contrary to what happens in the event of belief in bodies and their likeness to the senses) is that the operations of mathematics through which one describes the

7   Ibid., 14. Emphasis mine.

essences of things, remain true both in dreams and in waking. "For whether I am awake or asleep, two and three added together are five, and a square has no more than four sides."[8]

The withdrawal of the old self from the spontaneous faith in the trustworthiness of the senses until the last trenches of certainty that one comes to in analyzing the data of sensory experience has plotted a course clearly visible, familiar even, to the reader— it is that of knowledge by successive degrees of abstraction as theorized by Thomas Aquinas in the wake of Aristotle. One is able to abstract the general characteristics of bodies (head, hands, corporeal nature in general) from individual characteristics of individuated bodies perceived through the senses. It is the level of abstraction on which physics operates. From corporeal nature in general one can then separate the pure characteristics of the substance subjected to quantity with thought—figure, number, size: it is the plane of mathematics. Mathematics, in whose certainty the old self tries to encapsulate itself, is therefore the last frontier of knowledge deduced from the senses, and yet on this level of abstraction, thought places sensibility and the external world itself in parentheses and goes to work with pure concepts, exactly with those of mathematics. Thomas Aquinas speaks of "intelligible matter," with which mathematics works, obtained through abstraction from "sensible matter."[9]

The last refuge of the old self relies on all the previous levels of knowing derived from the senses for its firmness, or cohesiveness. If there are reasons to doubt all the beliefs derived from daily experience, and along with this experience all the sciences that deal with composite entities, such as physics, indubitability, and truth might find themselves in sciences that treat ultimate or final components, not in the end decomposable, of that experience, or rather of mathematics, that puts itself at the pinnacle of the process of abstraction accomplished through sensory data. Of course, mathematics is indifferent to the existence of an external

8   Ibid.
9   Thomas Aquinas. *Summa theologiae*, I, 85, ad 2.

world. Abandoning sciences that are based on the hypothesis of the existence of bodies outside the mind is therefore the price to be paid in order to find any propositions resistant to both reasons of doubt that have to do with the betrayal of the senses, as well as doubt that has to do with the dream theory.

But at this level it is no longer just the knowledge of the world of Aristotelian origin that is up for debate. The new science, in fact, maintains that sensory experience is purely subjective, and that that which is objective (that is, independent of the perceiving subject) sets off from this, are some initial elements (mathematical structures) that are not directly perceived by the senses, rather knowable by the intellect alone. Since the methodological work (unfinished), the *Regulae ad directionem ingenii,* Descartes speaks of "simple natures," the ultimate components of experienced reality, and identifies them in quantifiable properties.[10]

In this sense, one can say that Cartesian physics had already taken up the results of the early skeptical arguments of the first meditation. Hence, the new science is intangible with arguments of classical skepticism, each one a means of demonstrating the irrationality of trust in sensory experience, since even the dream theory, with what is ascertained by mathematical science, one finds to confirm the fact.

Precisely because doubts as to the trustworthiness of the senses and the possibility of dreams cannot eat away at Cartesian mathematics and science on which all of this founded, the true

10 Cf. The twelfth rule of the *Rule For the Direction of the Mind:* "That is why, since we are concerned here with things only in so far as they are perceived by the intellect, we term 'simple' only those things which we know so clearly and distinctly that they cannot be divided by the mind into others which are more distinctly known. Shape, extension and motion, etc. are of this sort; all the rest we conceive to be in a sense composed out of these." *The Philosophical Writings of Descartes, Volume I,* John Cottingham, *et al.,* 44. Experience is always constituted by entities composed of these natures, and so simple natures as such are never experienced. They are, however, individuated under the terms of a mental process of deconstructing the experience of concrete things.

foundational project of this Cartesian science begins now, in this moment when the indubitability of mathematical sciences is put to the test, that is, those sciences that have as their object rational foundation (simple natures) of sensory knowledge. The truth of mathematics depends only on the principle of non-contradiction, or else only on those laws which govern reasoning and thought. This is the sense of their independence from experience: only the analysis of mathematical propositions manifests their truth or falsity. That 2+3 equals five is true "both when I am sleeping and when I am awake" because its negation implies contradiction; theorems of geometrical figures are true because their negation would contradict the definition of that very same figure. Yet for the human mind it is impossible to conceive of the falsity of that whose contrary implies contradiction—hence, it is impossible to doubt the truth of mathematical propositions. This is why classical skepticism is stopped at the threshold of these sciences. If, as maintains classical skepticism, sensible certainty can be placed in doubt, but not mathematics, then a science that founded itself just on mathematics (as does Cartesian science) would have been declared up until this point.

Classical skepticism seems to be right: it is possible to doubt sensory experience, the existence of external objects and their likenesses to the sensations that they represent, yet it is not possible to doubt mathematical operations, such as the rules that govern thought. When one encounters propositions whose truth depends only on the principle of non-contradiction, one touches on the outer limits of human thought, and there is nowhere else to go beyond that. It would only be possible to doubt these propositions by altogether leaving human reason, and reason is unable to do this—therefore, and finally, one can say that mathematical science of the world, indifferent as it is to the existence of that which science is interested in, is absolutely certain and indubitable.

Nevertheless, the meditating self returns to object, saying that there is still a conceivable reason to doubt, albeit refined and very far from common sense, which threatens even mathematics, so that even mathematics needs a foundation: things that appear to be true to the human mind and that the human mind cannot successfully place in doubt, might appear false to some other mind. Despite the non-composite character of the natures that mathematics describes, even these could be false appearances like the composite bodies believed to be real. In such cases even mathematics could be a deceptive science as are those sciences that deal with composite things. There is, however, one difference. Until I concerned myself with composite things, I myself could have broken things down, coming to a deeper and "truer" level of these things. I could have broken down the painting into all of its primary colors. Instead, if even the simple natures were but appearances, I would have no way of breaking down this appearance to change it into something else, nor would I have any means to correct the error of these sciences which deal with the "most simple and general" natures. To subject mathematics to doubt, the instruments of classical skepticism are not enough, for they have exhausted their capacity to discuss the science of material things after having called into question sensory appearances. To exclude that mathematics is nothing other than deceitful appearances, I must first exclude the idea that the operations of reason, and thereby all those necessarily true propositions such as those of mathematics, may seem false to someone else's mind who has a deeper knowledge with respect to what is possessed by human reason.

There is but one being that human reason judges capable of pushing past reason itself, and it is that same being who made reason. By definition, then, this being is beyond human reason—it is God. An all-powerful God would be able to ensure that neither composite bodies nor simple natures exist outside of the mind. He would be able to make it so that the propositions of mathematics which the human mind cannot doubt might be false anyway. It is common experience that things which to some seem certain to others seem deceitful. Likewise, to an omnipotent God the mathematical operations that to me are indubitable might be in themselves fallacious. Every time I carry out some mathematical operation, I could be deceiving myself, as I am likewise capable of falling into error every time I judge the external reality of bodies. But in this case I would have no means of understanding the logic of deception. I do not know what it means to say that two and three do not make five, while I know very well what it means to say that bodies might not exist. Nevertheless, my reason which cannot comprehend how two and three might not make five is all the same capable of hypothesizing that to an all-powerful God, creator of my very reason, this same proposition is false. In this way a new skeptical argument reveals itself to be thinkable and operative, even though to classical skepticism it was inconceivable. Until this doubt is on its feet (and for Descartes this is the most interesting doubt, the only doubt capable of challenging the foundations of this science) one cannot say that mathematical operations, which I cannot but accept inasmuch as I cannot conceive of the contrary of that which I demonstrate through utilizing them, are true. As long as this motive of doubt remains thinkable, the certainty that occupies a human mind faced with analytically true propositions is merely psychological persuasion and not true science. If instead I was able to convince myself that that which the human mind is urged in an irresistible way to believe is true appears true to some other mind, well the indubitable will be declared true and I will have reached the "most perfect certainty."[11] I will have reached the science established as from the beginning absolutely true, and not just for the human mind.

This latter reason of doubting is justified by Descartes through an ancient thought, a *vetus opinio*. That is, justified by the thought of "an omnipotent God who made me the kind of creature that I am."[12] This God would have been able to want "go wrong every time I add two and three or count the sides of

11 This is the title Descartes gives the certainty that coincides with the truth. See "Replies to the Second Set of Set of Objections," in *The Philosophical Writings of Descartes, Volume II,* John Cottingham, *et al.*, 103.
12 Ibid.,14.

a square, or in some even simpler matter."[13] Nonetheless, the reasons for doubting the trustworthiness of reason extend beyond the theory of an all-powerful God and touch on the problem of the origin of my own being. If it were chance that produced my nature and not an all-powerful God, I would not then be able to free myself from the doubt of the falsity of those judgments that my nature irresistibly urges me to believe are true. For the more the cause of my nature is imperfect, the more probable it is that I deceive myself. The atheist, then, cannot hope to be exempted from the doubt of the validity of his own reason. The doubt we now find ourselves up against is the doubt surrounding the possibility that that which reason cannot but judge to be true (such as mathematical operations), might instead be false. Hence, modern science, which is built up presupposing the trustworthiness of mathematics, might in this case be unfounded.

1.3. *To Doubt the Indubitable*

Doubting propositions whose opposites imply contradiction seems to demand the impossible of the human mind: to doubt that which the mind is incapable of judging to be false. Descartes clarifies how it is that one might accomplish this in the beginning of the third meditation, and then later on in the fifth. There are propositions so simple and so obvious (such as basic mathematical operations) that the mind grasps them intuitively even after a quick first glance. It is not possible to doubt these directly, though it is possible to think that they might be false. That is, instead of considering each of them individually, one considers the possibility that an all-powerful God has thus created the human mind that each time the human mind assents to any proposition which cannot be conceived of as false it deceives itself. I am unable to think that two and three do not make five while I ponder it, and yet I am able to conceive of the proposition that "perhaps some God could have given me a nature such that I was deceived even in

13   Ibid.

matters which seemed most evident."[14] Or else I can conceive that what seems true to me appears to another mind as false. This possibility rests next to the incapacity to think that two and three might not make five, and makes it so that I must judge that the evidence of this proposition might be merely a psychological condition. That is, it is not enough to confirm that something not being dubious actually corresponds to the truth.

The irresistible assent to a proposition, in fact, is compatible with giving itself thinkable reasons on the basis of which that same proposition could be false and the evidence that accompanies it only apparent. When, however, the reasons for doubting hinge on propositions which are so simple that it makes it impossible to think of them as false, or doubt them, when they are in front of one's face, it is only possible to doubt those propositions indirectly under the category of "clear and distinct ideas."

Instead, to doubt complex reasoning and demonstrations it is enough to have in sight the conclusions of these demonstrations. One can step away from the actual sequence of the chain of these demonstrations, but always remembering to have once correctly conducted this series of demonstrations. In this case, the mind is not forced to assent (which is what happens when the mind is shown the simplest propositions) and it is thereby possible to think that for an all-powerful God the sum of the angles inside a triangle is not one hundred and eighty degrees, or that the demonstrations are false regardless of their validity. In both cases, it is necessary to disentangle oneself from the actual evidence for doubt to be psychologically possible even though it is the truth and the evidence itself that one doubts.

In order understand what it means to doubt actual evidence one must distinguish between the two levels of doubt: psychological doubt (the effective or actual act of doubting) and normative doubt (the presence of valid reasons for doubting). The presence of valid reasons for doubting is compatible with

14 *Meditations* in *The Philosophical Writings of Descartes, Volume II,* John Cottingham, *et al.*, III, 25.

impossibility of psychological doubt. Hence, psychologically it is impossible to doubt that two and three make five, or that three interior angles of a triangle are equal to two right angles when I undertake a demonstration of these. And yet there is a reason to think that all clear and distinct ideas (two plus three equals five, included) and the conclusions of demonstrations, even though conducted with precision, might still be false. This reason is not eliminated by the fact that, compared to individual propositions so simple that they can be grasped at a single glance or within the chain of demonstration, I am not able to think of them as false. This is why the indubitable character that emerges from the mind's gaze on simple propositions, and the entire chain of demonstration, cannot be accepted or taken as a sign of the truth of these propositions. The two meanings of doubtability do not overlap, but have between them an important relationship: if it is true that psychological indubitability is not sufficient to attest the absence of reasons for doubt, it is also true that when reasons for doubt come up, psychological doubt, in direct (complex demonstrations) or indirect (simple propositions) form must be possible. Only the complete absence of reasons to doubt is enough to produce a psychological incapacity to doubt in any applied condition and, conversely, a psychological incapacity to doubt in any given condition guarantees that there are no true reasons to doubt.

With the theory of an all-powerful God that might have condemned the human mind to irreversible error, one reaches the deepest layer of doubt—the doubt that gives thrust to the metaphysical undertaking in Cartesian science and compels one to address the existence and truthfulness of God. From this point on, Cartesian doubt no longer bears any likeness to classical skepticism. If anything, what we see in Descartes is the potential for skepticism in Christianity. In fact, it is actually Christianity that introduced the idea of the infinite divine potency on which all things depend. An all-powerful God might trick daily experience, make one see things that do not really exist, order to be righteous what the conscience marks as sinful, and even create false evidence in such a way that one readily assents to false propositions. Under the semblance of an all-powerful God, Christianity placed a character on the stage that could transform the most hardy theories of skepticism into reality, attributing to God the power to make the false seem absolutely true.

Now, as we know, Descartes takes the consequences of infinite divine potency very seriously, so much so that even against tradition he hypothesizes that the essences in mathematics were the fruits of divine creation. According to Descartes, God "just as he was free not to create the world, so he was no less free to make it untrue that all lines drawn from the center of a circle to the circumference are equal."[15] On the inside of this theory the possibility of urging doubt of mathematics, for the most part unspoken, was opened up. God could change the essences of mathematics though leaving the ideas of them unaltered, thereby rendering false what was true beforehand, and what still appears to be true. Nevertheless, as it is said in the *Meditations,* as in other organic developments of metaphysics, the silence on this doctrine is well-kept.

This silence is fully comprehensible in light of what we now know of the structure of this work. The doubt and adventure of doubting involve a human individual that is fed by the culture of the past, one that aspires "to become Descartes," but is not yet quite there, and hence doubt of mathematics can never be justified by the unspoken and absolutely innovative doctrines, as that of Descartes' free creation of eternal truths. Rather, to doubt mathematics, one will have to invoke an "ancient opinion," familiar to the old self, that of a God that is capable of everything, an opinion that stretches its roots down into the memory of the Scholastic arguments of the *potentia Dei,* particularly developed in the vein of Okham. In fact, in this context God was attributed with the capacity not to render what is true false, but to ensure that what is false *appears* to the human mind as necessarily true. On the heels of Descartes, an author he knew well, Francisco Suàrez, had

15   To Mersenne, 27 May 1630. *AT* I, 152. Cf. *K,* 15.

returned to this reflection posing the problem of how it might be possible to raise indubitability to be criterion for truth, since God, using his infinite potency could create necessary and invincible assent to what is false.[16]

The reasons for doubt that the old self is disposed to take into consideration also come from a culture of the past, and (as do beliefs that fall under their blows) are not fully founded on reason. One doubts of those ideas that are obscure and confused, as are confused the reasons of doubt that are opposed to them. Even mathematics, on the whole, is still surrounded by an aura of obscurity, for one does not know the full truth of its nature. It is, in fact, reached only through the process of abstraction by sensory data, as would say an Aristotelian, which in the course of the *Meditations* we know that its origin is in the baggage of innate ideas, as Plato maintains. It is only when the nature of mathematics is clarified that the implications of the hypothesis of divine deception will be fully known.

That the reasons for doubt are at times on account of a shroud of obscurity is particularly important for the most radical reason to doubt—the reason based on the notion of the infinitely powerful God. It is important that the hypothesis of a God who could have created the human mind false in its very make-up is shown to be the blossom of a *vetus opinio,* and not a clear and distinct idea. For as we shall see, this doubt will be eliminated the moment we come to a clear and distinct idea of God.[17] Descartes' strategy for demonstrating the falsity of the theory of the irreversible trickery or deception of reason (and therefore

16 F. Suàrez. *Disputationes Metaphysicae.* Disp. IX, II, VII.
17 Cf. Descartes to Buitendijck, 1643. *AT* IV, 64. "Not only is it illicit for the human mind to attribute something false to a God clearly and distinctly known, but *neither is it possible....* But to false gods ... constructed through the error of the human mind ... and even to the true God who is known only confusedly, is it good or bad to attribute something false, according to the motive behind this, the goodness or badness of the end involved with this motive." Cf. *K,* 145. Emphasis mine.

also the strategy for paving a passage from what is dubious to what is true) consists of the attempt to show that the theory of an all-powerful God who may have condemned the human mind to deception is conceivable only insofar as it is supported by an obscure and confused idea of God. When one arrives at a clear and distinct idea of God the proposition "an all-powerful God could have made me of such a nature that I am deceived even in that which I conceive of clearly and distinct" will seem contradictory, and thereby inconceivable. The clear and distinct ideas are then not doubtful in any aspect nor for any reason. One will then have reached the "most perfect certainty" and established the perfect science, a science safe from the objections of all skeptics. He who already possesses a clear and distinct idea of God, would from the outset discount the theory of a God using his power to make what is false seem true. For God would appear to him to be true as well as infinitely powerful. Instead, one is now dealing with reaching such an end, such a result as the truthfulness of God, by beginning with obscure ideas, with common sense "opinions," according to the intention of achieving persuasion through meditating.

Having taken such a long and arduous road to eliminate those reasons for doubt founded on the hypothesis of the deceiving God will not be for nothing, for in passing from confused knowledge of God to distinct knowledge of God other concepts will be clarified. First among these is the nature of the mind. Philosophy of mathematics will also shift, from the initial Aristotelianism to the Platonized notion expounded upon in the fifth meditation. Hence the meditative agenda will lead the forward charge of the project to found the certainty of reason along with the construction of the new science.

Yet let us return to the meditating self: opinions, or thoughts, which have been placed in doubt up to now are still highly probable, and this very probability will once again impose itself on the mind, as soon as stop contemplating the reasons put into play to justify the negation of these opinions. The old self is always lurking, made strong in the forcefulness of the power of custom wherein the mind tends to retreat in its search of repose, fatigued by the effort to distance from it all beliefs in which it has for a long time trusted. In order to maintain the *epoché* of all prior beliefs, Descartes introduces the idea of a "lesser" divinity, an evil genius "of the utmost power and cunning who has employed all his energies in order to deceive me."[18] The evil genius takes upon himself all the prior grounds for doubt regarding the existence of anything external to the mind and thereby dispenses from having to remember them one by one. "I shall think that the sky, the air, the earth, colours, shapes, sounds and all external things are merely the delusions of dreams which he has devised to ensnare my judgment. I shall consider myself as not having hands or eyes, or flesh, or blood or senses, but as falsely believing that I have all these things."[19] It is about personifying the whole of the skeptic's argument in a less disturbing figure, and one less subject to the theological objections of an omnipotent God. It is thereby more easily thinkable, or feasible. On the whole, even Suárez, after having raised the doubt that an omnipotent God had created an irresistible attachment to what is false, introduced a less demanding theory, one concerning the "evil angel," or rather a demon who induces one into false beliefs through tricks and deception.[20] Having an evil genius permits the undertaking of research safe from the allure of ancient ideas, as this evil genius is the countering force to the tendency to fall back into the tangle of normal beliefs. And so the mind, in its freedom, will be able to assume "all the things about whose existence it can have even the slightest doubt"[21] do not actually exist. In the void or emptiness caused by this, the mind can now begin its search for the indubitable foundation of science.

18 *Meditations* in *The Philosophical Writings of Descartes Volume II,* John Cottingham, *et al.*, I, 15.
19 Ibid.
20 F. Suárez, *Disputationes Metaphysicae*, Disp. IX, II, VII.
21 "Synopsis" in *Meditations* in *The Philosophical Writings of Descartes, Volume II,* John Cottingham, *et al.*, 9.

2. The Existence and Nature of the Self

As indicated in the title, the second meditation proposes to demonstrate what the nature of the human mind is and that it is easier to know this particular nature than the nature of bodies. It literally reads, "The Nature of the Human Mind, and How It Is Better Known than the Body." Surprisingly, the title leaves out perhaps the most well known Cartesian argument surrounding the achievement of the most basal certainty—the certainty of the existence of the self, or one's own existence. This is immortalized in the formula *cogito, ergo sum,* or simply the *cogito* in its abbreviated form. The title emphasizes instead the parts of the meditations that constitute the basis for his refutation of empiricism and for the possibility of a new science. That is, it makes way for the possibility that knowledge of the mind might be independent from knowledge of bodies. The second meditation reads like a kind of layered edifice built around the problem of modern science. The first and original truth, that one knows he exists (the existence of one's self), provides the basis for the absolute certainty of this science. The investigation of the nature of the self and the possibility of knowing it independently of knowledge of bodies sets up instead the foundation for the refutation of empiricism. In the end, on the inside of this two-tiered approach to the foundation of science, Descartes begins to erect the very content of physics, providing the first elements of knowledge of the nature of bodies.

Ideally, we can divide the second meditation into three parts. In the first part one comes to primal certainty, or the certainty of the existence of the self. In the second part one pursues the nature of the self. In the third part, it is demonstrated that the mind is more easily known than the body.

2.1. *The Existence of the Self (That I Exist)*

Doubt, then, places the existence of all things in parenthesis, even the existence of the meditator's body. In this universal *epoché*, before resigning himself to the fact and admitting that nothing in the world can be held as certain, the self once again tries to find the indubitable proposition. He is looking for something that, like the Archimedean point, would be the cornerstone in the construction of untouchable certainties, and this, at the conclusion of an intense interrogation of the meditating self with himself, is what will be traced back to the proposition "I am, I exist."

> Am not I, at least, something? But I have just said that I have no senses and no body. This is the sticking point: what follows from this? Am I not so bound up with a body and with senses that I cannot exist without them? But I have convinced myself that there is absolutely nothing in the world, no sky, no earth, no minds, no bodies. Does it follow that I too do not exist? No: if I convinced myself of something then I certainly existed. But there is a deceiver of supreme power and cunning who is deliberately and constantly deceiving me. In that case I too undoubtedly exist, if he is deceiving me; and let him deceive me as much as he can, he will never bring it about that I am nothing so long as I think that I am something. So after considering everything very thoroughly, I must finally conclude that this proposition, *I am, I exist,* is necessarily true whenever it is put forward by me or conceived in my mind.[22]

The proposition "I am, I exist" withstands all doubt, even if there is some "all-powerful and very astute" being who deceives me, since the existence of one's self is a condition for doubt ("I existed without a doubt if I am convinced of something or even if I simply think of something"), as well as for deception ("There is no doubt that I exist if the deceiving being is in fact deceiving me"). Hence, the hypothesis that I am being deceived attests to the fact of my existence rather than renders it doubtful. The green light given to the advancement of a proposition that affirms the

22 *Mediations* in The Philosophical Writings of Descartes, Volume II, John Cottingham, *et al.*, II, 17.

existence of the self stems from the impossibility of coming up with a premise in the first person singular, which does not confirm it. Existence is implied rather than excluded even in the very thought of being deceived. In the *cogito* for the first time one reaches the meeting place of psychological and normative resilience to doubt. There is no reason for which doubt can undermine the certainty of the premise "I exist," if it is I myself to think it.

In the *Meditations,* the first indubitable premise is *I am, I exist* and not the famous formula *I think, therefore I am* that Descartes uses in the *Discourse on the Method* and to which he will return to in his *Principles of Philosophy.* The formula of the *Meditations* relegates thinking to second place and infers the existence of the self directly by doubt, though he immediately restores the dependence of certainty of one's being on thought. The saying *Ego sum, ego existo* is true "each and every time that (...) I *conceive of it* in my mind ... I am, I exist—that is certain. But for how long? For as long *as I am thinking.*"[23] On this point Descartes is exceptionally clear in his replies to Gassendi's objections. Gassendi does not see the necessity of proposing thought as a condition in reaching the certainty of one's existence, for this might be equally witnessed by any other activity of the self. The *cogito, sum* could be substituted by "I walk, therefore I exist." Descartes flatly denies this possibility. One cannot be certain of actually walking (one could be dreaming), nor certain of the consequence Gassendi wants draw from this, that "I exist." "This inference [I am walking, therefore I exist] is certain only if it applies to this awareness, and not to the movement of the body which sometimes—in the case of dreams—is not occurring at all, despite the fact that I seem to myself to be walking. Hence from the fact that I think I am walking I can very well infer the existence of a mind which as this thought, but not the existence of a body that walks. And the same applies in other cases."[24] This reply makes it very clear to us that

23 Ibid., 18.
24 "Replies to the Fifth Set of Set of Objections," in *The Philosophical Writings of Descartes, Volume II,* John Cottingham, *et al.*, 244.

for Descartes thinking is the only activity that attests to the existence of the self in an indubitable way, as well as the fact that thought is implied in any activity of the self. One cannot doubt the existence of one's self if it is derived from the *thought* of taking a stroll, because in this case the premise is indubitable. It is not indubitable if derived from the activity of walking insofar as one can doubt the truth of this premise, that is, to have doubts about the actual walking. Even doubting the fact of being deceived manifests the existence of one's self, for doubt itself is a thought and it is never possible to doubt the fact of one's own thought. The content of thought (or, as we shall see later, of judgments) might be totally false, but certainty of the fact that I am thinking can never be false.

The argumentation through which Descartes claims the indubitable character of one's own existence looks like a classic argument of the proof of the validity of the first principles. The first principles, precisely because they are such, cannot be demonstrated nor derived from something else. If by chance someone were to deny these it would not then be possible to convince him of his error through some demonstration. The occasion for urging him to concede the validity of the first principles which he denies consists of showing him how this very negation of his instead implies the confirmation of the first principles. Aristotle uses a line of reasoning similar to this (a proof by confutation of the theory of an opponent) to defend the necessity of the principle of non-contradiction. The test of the firmness of the *cogito, sum,* even in the deception theory, reminds the reader of this same process. Instead of *I think, therefore I am,* I might say *I think that I do not exist* but all the same I ought to concede that I must exist, if in the end I am thinking that I do not exist. The existence of the self is verified even in negation if it is carried out by the same thinking subject.

The procedure itself through which the proposition *I think, therefore I exist* is ascertained seems, then, to fall back on its indemonstrability, consistent with its function as first principle on which the whole edifice of science must be built. Later on,

Descartes has the opportunity to clarify his thought on this point when he discusses the objections of his interlocutors.

Descartes is primarily concerned with unhinging the theory that would render the existence of the self the conclusion of a syllogism of which "I think" is the minor premise and the major premise is "All things that think are, or exist." If this were true, the proposition *I think, therefore I am* would not be the first certain proposition, for it would depend on a more general one that would act as the premise. This objection demands that the proposition *cogito, sum* be the conclusion of a syllogism similar to the following:

All that which thinks, exists.
I think.
Therefore, I exist.

But Descartes has always denied that things are so. "And when we become aware that we are thinking things, this is a *primary notion* which is not derived by means of any syllogism. When someone says, 'I am thinking, therefore I am, or I exist,' he does not deduce existence from thought by means of a syllogism, but recognizes it as something *self-evident* by a simple intuition of the mind."[25] Nevertheless, Descartes has also admitted that, according to logical coherency, the general principle "in order to think it is necessary to exist" precedes the truth of the proposition *I think, I am.* "And when I said that the proposition *I am thinking, therefore I exist* is the first and most certain of all to occur to anyone who philosophizes in an orderly way, I did not in saying that deny that one must first know (...) that it is impossible that that which thinks should not exist, and so forth."[26] Here Descartes seems to uphold two incompatible positions. One, that the *cogito* is the first principle, but, two, it depends on something else, another principle.

25 "Replies to the Second Set of Objections," in *The Philosophical Writings of Descartes, Volume II,* John Cottingham, *et al.,* 100. Emphasis mine.
26 Cf. *Principles of Philosophy.* I, § 10, in *The Philosophical Writings of Descartes, Volume I.* John Cottingham, *et al.,* 196.

An initial avenue towards the reconciliation of Descartes' contrasting affirmations passes through the distinction between the analytic and synthetic method. The discovery of one's own existence follows the usual way of discovery of any truth. "If we are to discover the truth," Descartes explains to Gassendi, "it is certain that we must always begin with particular notions in order to arrive at general ones later on (though we may also reverse the order and deduce other particular truths once we have discovered general ones). Thus when we teach a child the elements of geometry we will not be able to get him to understand the general proposition 'When equal quantities are taken from equal amounts the remaining amounts will be equal,' or 'The whole is greater than its parts,' unless we show him examples in particular cases."[27] That the cake is bigger than one of its slices is true because the principle "the whole is greater than its parts" holds fast. Yet the child might ignore the principle and still clearly understand its example. From here the child can easily trace back to certain knowledge of the principle. Hence, according to the order of the discovery, *I think, therefore I am* is known first and independently from the general principle "to think it is necessary to exist," which in any case is derived from the former.

It is, then, firstly the logic of the analytic method which excludes the syllogistic interpretation of the *cogito*. But it would be reductive to limit oneself to the invocation of the analytic method to justify the autonomy of the *cogito, sum* from the general principle "to think it is necessary to exist." An illuminating clarification in this case is to be found in a letter addressed to Clerselier. "The word 'principle' can be understood in varying senses. One is searching for a 'common notion' that is so clear and so universal that it is able to act as a principle in proving the existence of all (...) the 'beings' that are known after it. It is another thing to seek after 'a Being' whose existence may be known more than that of all others, in such a way that this serves as a

---

27 "Replies to the Fifth Set of Objections," in *The Philosophical Writings of Descartes, Volume II*, John Cottingham, *et al.*, 271.

principle by which to know others (...) In [this] sense, the first principle is that 'our Soul exists,' for there is nothing whose existence is more noted."[28]

If one utilizes the principle "to think I must exist" as a premise in demonstrating the existence of one's self, the existence of the self is herein deduced as the existence of an individual being, such as that of Peter in a syllogism similar to the following:

> To think it is necessary to exist.
> Peter thinks.
> Therefore, Peter exists.

In this syllogism one might doubt the minor premise, that is, the fact that Peter is thinking, and so then doubt that Peter exists. Instead, when the syllogism has to do with one's own existence it is impossible to harbor doubts about the conclusion "I exist" because, indeed, it depends on the minor premise "I think." And it is impossible to doubt this. If, however, one moves to the minor premise, to the "I think," the deduction of one's own existence no longer requires the premise "to think it is necessary to exist" because existence is immediately intuited without any reasoning required. In the case of the existence of the self the major premise cannot explain the indubitable character of one's own existence. Rather, what explains it, the minor premise, renders the major premise meaningless in that it gives witness to the existence of the thinking subject on its own. The reduction of the *cogito, sum* to a syllogism is possible in the order of logic because the principle "to think it is necessary to exist" is already implicit in the proposition "If I think, I exist." This is similar to the proposition "If Peter thinks, Peter exists," and once reduced to a syllogism the *cogito,* the existence of one's self, like that of Peter, follows the principle "to think it is necessary to exist." Nonetheless, its placement in syllogistic form is misleading in that it hides the peculiarity of the Cartesian principle. That is, that it singles out a *more* certain existence than that of any other being. This heightened certainty

28   Descartes to Clerselier, June 1646. *AT,* 444. Cf. *K,* 197.

would be masked rather than displayed if the proposition *I think, I exist* were deduced from the general principle "to think it is necessary to exist." The indubitable nature of the existence of one's self is obtained through a procedure that cannot be repeated for other existing—albeit thinking—beings.

The young Descartes fiercely disapproved of the dialecticians who entrust the search for truth to the rules of inference. "But to make it even clearer that the aforementioned art of reasoning contributes nothing whatsoever to knowledge of the truth, we should realize that, on the basis of their method, dialecticians are unable to formulate a syllogism with a true conclusion unless they are already in possession of the substance of the conclusion, i.e., unless they have previous knowledge of the very truth deduced in the syllogism. It is obvious therefore that they themselves can learn nothing new from such forms of reasoning, and hence that ordinary dialectic is of no use whatever to those who wish to investigate the truth of things."[29] This is particularly evident in the case of the existence of one's self. The syllogism,

> To think it is necessary to exist.
> I think.
> Therefore, I exist.

is true only if it is true that I am thinking. But if it happens that I am thinking, I still already know that I exist. The possibility of

---

[29] *Rules for the Direction of the Mind*, in *The Philosophical Writings of Descartes, Volume I*. John Cottingham, *et al.*, 36–37. Cf. the tenth rule. In the paragraph wherein Descartes concedes that knowledge of the principle, "in order to think it is necessary to exist," precedes the truth of the *cogito*, he strongly discourages one from embarking on the path of using the ordering of logical precedence. For in such a procedure one would lose sight of the very thing he wants to demonstrate, something that is considered in and of itself. "I have often noticed that philosophers make the mistake of employing logical definitions in an attempt to explain what was already simple and self-evident; the result is that they only make matters more obscure." *Principles* I, § 10, in *The Philosophical Writings of Descartes, Volume I*. John Cottingham, *et al.*, 195–196.

demonstrating the existence of one's self in a syllogistic way depends on the ascertained truth of the existence of one's self.

For the greatest certainty with respect to every other existence, the existence of one's self is a first principle in what concerns the construction of a science. This is why Descartes likens it to the axioms, what is known as primary and "without which [the mind] would not be able to reason."[30] Yet the *cogito* has a peculiarity that the other principles do not have, the principle "to think it is necessary to exist" included. Descartes says repeatedly that no first principle can say anything about reality outside the mind. Therefore, the axioms, though being indubitable do not produce true knowledge and the knowledge proper to them "is not normally called a science by the dialecticians."[31] This is why, as he

---

30 To Sihon, March or April 1648, *AT* V, 137–38. See also "Replies to Second Set of Objections," in *The Philosophical Writings of Descartes, Volume II,* John Cottingham, *et al.*, 100: "When I said that we can know nothing for certain until we are aware that God exists, I expressly declared that I was speaking only of knowledge of those conclusions which can be recalled when we are no longer attending to the arguments by means of which we deduced them. Now awareness of first principles is not normally called 'knowledge' by dialecticians. And when we become aware that we are thinking things, this is a primary notion which is not derived by means of any syllogism. When someone says, 'I am thinking, therefore I am, or exist', he does not deduce existence from thought by means of a syllogism, but recognizes it as something self-evident by a simple intuition of the mind. This is clear from the fact that if he were deducing it by means of a syllogism, he would have to have previous knowledge of the major premise 'Everything which thinks is, or exists'; yet in fact he learns it from experiencing in his own case that it is impossible that he should think without existing. It is in the nature of our mind construct general propositions on the basis of our knowledge of particular ones." Emphasis mine.

31 Ibid., In *Principles of Philosophy,* I §§ 48, 49 Descartes distinguishes between those propositions which concern "things" from those having to do with "eternal truths" which do not have existential implications. "All the objects of our perception we regard either as things, or affections of things, or else as eternal truths which have

says to Clerselier, these do not render us "more wise."[32] On the contrary, the *cogito, sum,* unique among the other principles, proposes the existence of something—the existence of the "I," or one's self. Therefore, the *cogito* and only the *cogito* can be the Archimedean point for any reconstruction of science. For with the *cogito* we are already inside the realm of true knowledge of things.

The intention of presenting the *cogito* as a first principle is evident in the insistence of its intuitive character, despite the fact that some formulations might describe it as a kind of reasoning ("I think, *therefore* I am). Descartes expresses this in a letter to an unknown correspondent. "This knowledge ('I think, therefore I am') is not a product of our reasoning (...) our mind sees it, senses it, wields it."[33] In this letter Descartes utilizes as the most basic truth the formula already present in the *Discourses* as well as in the *Principles,* that leads one to think of existence as an inferred thought (again, "I think, *therefore* I am"). Yet in the meantime, Descartes denies this proposition is entirely a fruit of one's reasoning. To denote the kind of knowledge that the *cogito* refers to Descartes uses the verb "to sense."[34] That is, he chooses the verb that, as opposed to those signifying "to reason," "to infer," "to

no existence outside our thought," in *The Philosophical Writings of Descartes, Volume I.* John Cottingham, *et al.,* 208. See also § 49: "But when we recognize that it is impossible for anything to come from nothing, the proposition *Nothing comes from nothing* is regarded not as a really existing thing, or even as a mode of a thing, but as an eternal truth which resides within our mind. Such truths are termed common notions or axioms." Ibid., 209.

32 To Clerselier, June or July 1646. *AT* IV, 444. Cf. *K,* 197.

33 Unknown but thought to be, Descartes to Silhon, 1648. *AT* V, 137–38. "Would you not concede that perhaps you are less certain of the presence of the things you see, inasmuch as you might not be in line with this proposition, 'I think, therefore I am'? This knowledge is in no way the fruit of our own reasoning, neither is it something imparted to us by our teachers. The mind sees it, feels it, wields it. And ... it provides you with ... proof of your capacity to receive from God in your soul's intuitive knowledge."

34 *Translator's Note:* The verb in French is *sentir.*

deduce," excludes the relevance of inferential reasoning. He has already expressed himself along these lines in analogous terms in his reply to the second objections. "Yet in fact he learns it from experiencing in his own case that it is impossible that he should think without existing."[35] This justifies the absence of any and all linguistic references to the deductive form "I am, I exist" in the *Meditations*. The "feel" or "sense" as opposed to "reason" indicates that the certainty of one's existence derives from direct experience, a primary and original intuition, so much so that, in the letter just cited, Descartes compares it to the Beatific vision of God. The *cogito, sum* might be translated as "I experience existing in the act of thinking." On the whole, the theory according to which intuition, with which the first principles are apprehended (as opposed to deduction), is never deceitful, has already been claimed by, among others, Thomas Aquinas.[36] Descartes refastens himself to this tradition insisting on the comparison between the *cogito* and the axioms—it is intuitively certain and it is not possible to deny it without in reality confirming it—and herein lies the ultimate reason for its resistance to any reason for doubt.

How it might be possible that the apparent deduction of existence from thought is instead an experience of one's own existence in the act of thinking is better understood if one admits that even here there is already at work the identification of thought with conscious activity. This "identification" becomes explicit in the replies to the second objections.[37] The fact that thought is always conscious activity allows Descartes to transform the experience of existence into an experience of the existence of one's self, the "I"

---

35 "Replies to the Second Set of Objections," in *The Philosophical Writings of Descartes, Volume II*, John Cottingham, *et al.*100.

36 Cf. Thomas Aquinas. *Summa theologiae*. I, 58, 5.

37 Cf. "Replies to the Second Set of Objections," in *The Philosophical Writings of Descartes, Volume II*. John Cottingham, *et al.*, 113: "*Thought*. I use this term to include everything that is within us in such a way that we are immediately aware of it. Thus all operations of the will, the intellect, the imagination and the senses are thoughts." See also, *Principles of Philosophy* I, § 9, in *The*

who thinks. One is conscious of existing. For this reason there is no "passage" from thought to existence, but only experience of one's own existence through thought. Strictly speaking, it is not the proposition "I exist" that is intuited as true, but the entire proposition "I think, therefore I exist" that is the object of intuition. As Spinoza will later ink, "'I think, therefore I am' is a single proposition equivalent to this: 'I am one who thinks.'"[38]

Experience of one's existence in thought, or through thought, renders it indubitable, but also marks the limits of primary, or the most original, certainty. He who might hear me declare the proposition "I think, therefore I am" would not for this be unable to doubt my existence since he could have dreamt that he heard me speak these words. Absolute certainty of one's existence is not inter-subjective (it is not translatable). And not only this, the certainty of one's own existence is not a stable acquisition, rather limited to the moment in which the thought occurs, or the activity of thought occurs: "I am, I exist—that is certain. But for how long? For as long as I am thinking. For it could be that were I totally to cease from thinking, I should totally cease to exist."[39] On the basis of this, which as a foundation is absolutely solid (though only for the one who experiences it and limited to the moment in which it is experienced), Descartes means to commence the construction of the certainty of science.

2.2. *The Nature of the Self*

As it would be an error to liken Cartesian doubt in the first meditation to classical skepticism, it is likewise erroneous to consider the revival of skeptical arguments against sensible knowledge as a formality that has nothing to do with the Cartesian

> *Philosophical Writings of Descartes, Volume II.* John Cottingham, *et al.*, 195: "By the term 'thought,' I understand everything which we are aware of as happening within us, in so far as we have awareness of it."

38 Baruch Spinoza, *Descartes' Principles of Philosophy*. Prolegomenon (Part I).

39 *Meditations* in *The Philosophical Writings of Descartes, Volume II,* John Cottingham, *et al.*, II, 18.

enterprise. It is actually extremely important to assay the possibility of knowledge independent from the existence of bodies (an existence placed in parenthesis thanks to hyperbolic doubt) in that defeating Aristotelian science requires this possibility. The question as to what one can know from within the theory of annihilation of the external world and one's body takes on the role of a absolutely crucial experience for the foundation of the new science.

According to the theory of knowledge in the Aristotelian-Scholastic tradition, if bodies did not exist, strictly speaking one would not be capable of knowing anything, not even one's own mind, for all knowledge begins with the perception of bodies. Descartes has already shown how at least certainty of the existence of one's self might be independent from the existence of bodies. From here until the beginning of the sixth meditation, Descartes devotes himself to toppling the pillars of empiricism. He demonstrates how the mind can come to the fundamental truth of itself, and indeed of matter, even if bodies did not exist. That is, the mind can truthfully know the nature and properties pertaining to matter. It ends up being that the existence of bodies is a detail philosophers and scientists can pass over as it is the last thing they should worry about inasmuch as all of science and its foundation are realized not knowing whether bodies, including one's own, exist.

Founding the certainty of science on the certainty of one's own existence is an absolute novelty in philosophical thought. Nevertheless, the position claiming that the existence of one's self is a part of every act of thought (hence indubitable) is not invented by, or original to, Descartes. Arnauld, author of the fourth objections, calls to mind Saint Augustine. But even in the Aristotelian-Scholastic tradition one can find something similar. On one occasion Thomas wrote, "no one can consent to the notion that he does not exist. For in thinking anything, he perceives to exist."[40] On the whole, Descartes never stresses the originality of his argument. "It is something of itself so simple and so natural to infer that one exists from the fact that one doubts, that it could

---

40   Thomas Aquinas, *De veritate,* Q. 10, art. 12, ad. 7.

have been penned by anyone."[41] What flat-out breaks with the Aristotelian tradition is instead the theory that Descartes comes up with immediately following the certainty of his own existence—that the nature of one's self consists only of thought and one can come to know of it independently from the existence of bodies.

Descartes facilitates an encounter with empiricism and announces the total overturning of its positions. He declares that not only is the mind known independently from the body, but it is known in a better way than bodies are known. Not only is the mind known prior to bodies, but the experience of bodies depends on the nature of the mind.

The first stage of Descartes' counter-empiricist revolution consists of determining the nature of one's self independently from the existence of bodies. First of all, and according to the rules of meditating, Descartes looks for hints in the traditional thoughts and "prejudices" of his own nature in establishing what truly belongs to him. If pressed to speak on what belongs to the nature of one's self, before embarking on the adventure of doubt, Descartes, playing the part of the average cultured man, would have attributed to it some corporeal characteristics (such as having members or parts) and would have considered his own body as likened to a corpse. That is, deprived of any vital function inasmuch as it is barely a body. Vital functions, sensitive and intellectual, would actually be referred to the soul. The attribution of vital functions to the soul is originally Aristotelian,[42] and Descartes takes it to be a spontaneous belief, on the basis of the most reiterated theory that maintains Aristotelian science is simply a systematization of common sense (or, the popular and unfounded beliefs). Pressed to speak on the nature of the soul, Descartes would have realized that he never makes that an object of thorough investigation. He would have imagined it to be a thin or fragile body, ethereal like

41 Descartes to unknown recipient, November 1640. *AT* III, 248.
42 Aristotle, *De anima*, II, 2, 413b. "The soul is the principle of the aforementioned functions and is defined by them. That is, defined by the vegetative, sensitive, and rational functions, and then by movement."

wind or like fire. Here Descartes attributes the theories of the nature of the soul originating in the Stoics and Epicureans to common sense. They are vague and inadequately developed opinions: "Yet I did not dwell on what it is, the soul." On the other hand, he would declare himself to be convinced of knowing in great detail the nature of the body. "In what regards the body, I did not doubt its nature at all. I thought I knew it quite distinctly." The body is an extended thing, figurable, impenetrable, mobile, etc. Hence, tradition presents the scenario in which the body is the favored object of investigation and maintains that it might be better known than the mind, though one does not actually have a sufficiently defined position regarding the nature of the mind.

There is no doubt that at the height of the second meditation the question of the nature of one's self has to be made separately from the knowledge of bodies. Knowledge of bodies, in fact, is theoretically eliminated by the presence of the evil genius. One could say that in this situation it is impossible to determine the nature of one's self and one must be satisfied simply with its existence. But it is not so, for if the characteristic of one's self that allows it to be known as existing is uncovered, this same characteristic will reveal the nature of the self as well. The categories that guide Cartesian reasoning have to do with the notion, moreover made explicit here, of substance and the principal attribute which constitutes the nature of any substance. A substance is something that "is a complete thing,"[43] and so it does not need something else in order to subsist. A substance is never known through itself, but always through one or more attributes that inhere in the substance and constitute its nature.[44] If I know enough about a characteristic of some being that I thereby know that that being can exist "by itself," or independently from another being, I know that that

43 "Replies to the Fourth Set of Objections," in *The Philosophical Writings of Descartes, Volume II*, John Cottingham, *et al.*, 156.
44 Ibid. "We do not have immediate knowledge of substances, as I have noted elsewhere. We know them only by perceiving certain forms or attributes which must inhere in something if they are to exist; and we call the thing in which they inhere a 'substance'."

being is a substance. Furthermore, that characteristic which led me to this conclusion constitutes the nature of that substance. But I know that I exist and that thought, and only thought, allows me to say this about myself. Knowledge of the existence of one's self does not depend on the body nor the functions traditionally attributed to the soul, functions that require the presence of bodies in order to be carried out, functions such as those called vegetative and sensitive. Essentially, I can overlook these activities and continue to be convinced of existing. Thought, however, is a necessary condition and sufficient to know that one's self exists. "'I am, I exist,' this is certain. But for how long? Indeed, for as long as I am thinking." Realizing this, Descartes derives a conclusion regarding the nature of one's self: since it is thought that makes known the capacity of one's self to subsist independently of all else, thought is known as the principal attribute (the essence) of one's self. I know myself as a *thing* (*res*) that thinks. Even though here Descartes never uses the term "substance," the term "thing" expresses the same idea. The idea that Descartes wants to drive home through an analysis of the proposition "I think, I exist" is quite demanding. I know myself as a substance whose nature is constituted by thought alone, in total opposition to the Aristotelian position which holds that human substance is a composite of form (the soul) and matter (the body). But it also goes against all Stoic and Epicurean concepts of the soul that present the soul as a thin or fragile body, like wind or a flame. Together with the existence of one's self, the first indubitable proposition furthermore reveals its nature.

In his replies to the objections, Descartes clarifies himself on this point, first to Caterus and then more broadly to Arnauld. Descartes' argument does not end with corporality not belonging to one's self, in that one's self is conceived of without thinking of the body, or even thinking that any bodies exist. Formulated in this way, the argument seems quite weak. I can conceive of a geometric figure while ignoring or denying various properties even though they actually belong to its nature. If I were to conclude that these properties do not belong to the nature of that figure because I conceived of it apart from these, I am drawing my conclusion on the basis of imperfect knowledge. Arnauld elaborates on an observation of this kind in the following comparison. It is possible to obtain an adequate definition of a triangle while ignoring some properties of a triangle, or even denying them altogether. On the basis of Descartes' theory, however, one would have to conclude that these do not belong to the nature of a triangle. This would be an erroneous conclusion. "But how is my perception of the nature of my mind any clearer than his perception of the nature of the triangle?"[45] Perhaps, though having a correct definition of the mind as a thinking thing, while overlooking various properties that belong to its nature, it is on account of such ignorance that I can affirm that the nature of the mind consists *only* in thought. But the force of the Cartesian argument lies in the fact that attributing to it thought alone one's self is clearly and distinctly conceived of *as a complete thing*. A thing is conceived of as complete when one conceives that it can subsist on its own by way of some of its characteristics. That is, it is complete when it is properly conceived of as a substance. The argument by which one proves that the body does not belong to the nature of one's self is *not* the following: I clearly and distinctly conceive of *my own self without the body,* therefore I know that corporality does not belong to the nature of my own self. Instead the argument should read as follows: I clearly and distinctly conceive that *I can subsist without the body,* therefore I conceive of my own self as a complete thing, or a substance, without the body. Therefore, I conceive that corporality does not belong to the nature of my own self.

Furthermore, it is not necessary that knowledge of one's self cover all of its characteristics (that is, that it be *complete knowledge*) to establish that corporality does not belong to its nature. If it were so, we would never know the nature of anything. It can very well happen that the finite mind has complete knowledge of something, but it would never be aware of this fact. Only God who knows his own potency through which he made things knows fully what is contained therein and all of their properties. If complete

45   Ibid., 142.

knowledge of a being were necessary to know its nature, we would never be really certain of knowing anything. For the conclusion that Descartes intends to draw from the nature of one's self it is enough to have knowledge regarding those characteristics that reveal the capacity of a being to subsist on its own and independently of all else (or knowledge that that being is a *complete thing*). Now, thought is the characteristic that reveals the substantial character of one's self. Thought is the necessary and sufficient condition to know its existence, hence it constitutes its nature, and regardless of the relationship it might have with the body. Perhaps I do not know all the properties of my own self, but I do know that no later-discovered property is essential to it.[46] With that, Descartes sets up the first step in the reasoning that will lead him to conclude that between the mind and the body there is the strongest kind of distinction in force—that is, real distinction. Real distinction is what runs between two substances that can subsist independently from one another, while the modal distinction, or the distinction that runs between a substance and its various modes, is not reciprocal. A substance can subsist independently from each of its modes (but not without the modes of the whole—for example, extension can take any form but it nevertheless must always have one), while its modes cannot subsist without the substance.

In his summary of the *Meditations,* Descartes clarifies that the real distinction between the body and the soul is wholly proved in the second, fifth, and sixth meditations. Essentially, merely knowing the nature and existence of the body, which is the object of the fifth and sixth meditations, leads one to conclude that not only the mind is conceivable as a thing in itself apart from the body, but the same holds true for the body in relation to the mind. In the fifth

46 As Descartes explains to Arnauld: "Yet since that of which I am aware is sufficient to enable me to subsist with it and it alone, I am certain that I could have been created by God without having these other attributes of which I am unaware, and hence that these other attributes do not belong to the essence of the mind." See "Replies to the Fourth Set of Objections," in *The Philosophical Writings of Descartes, Volume II,* John Cottingham, *et al.,* 155.

and sixth meditations we come to see that *both* the body and the mind are conceived of as individual substances (again, independent from one another). Knowledge of the nature of the body thereby offers proof of what we already know in the wake of knowledge of the nature of the mind, obtained in the second meditation. The mind can be conceived of as a thing complete even without the body, for indeed thought alone makes it known as something capable of existing independently of the other.

But knowledge of the nature and existence of the body bears one single verification, even though extremely meaningful, of the fact that in the knowledge one has of it, the nature of the mind consists *solely* in thought. As early as the second meditation one conceives of the mind as a substance capable of subsisting on the sheer force of thought, and likewise independently from the relations it has with anything else. That is, as early as the second meditation one can exclude that whatever relation the mind enters into with the body, such a relation might be judged to be essential to the nature of the mind. At this point we can exclude that the nature of one's self consists of its corporality and that the mind is a mode of the body (otherwise I could not conceive of it to be able to subsist without the body).

The conclusions that are already legitimately deduced based on the knowledge one has of one's self nevertheless do not yet allow the assertion that since *I know my own self* clearly and distinctly as something complete by way of thought alone, *I am in reality* a thinking substance whose nature consists *only* in thinking. From this latter conclusion the hypothesis, still in play, of the infinitely powerful God who could have constructed my mind as naturally inclined to error and who prohibits the use of clear and distinct knowledge as a mark of the truth, leaves me divided. This is the real reason why the demonstration that the nature of one's self consists in mere thought cannot claim to be accomplished in the second meditation. Until the hypothesis and the threat of divine deception are in play, I would only be able to affirm that I *know* my own self as a substance whose essence consists of the activity of thinking, but not that *I really am* for I do not yet know whether the ordering of my thoughts corresponds to reality or not. To be able to affirm that in reality there corresponds a substance whose nature is simply thought to the knowledge of the existence of the mind as a substance separate from the body, I must first see to a demonstration of divine truthfulness. "And yet may it not perhaps be the case that these very things which I am supposing to be nothing, because they are unknown to me, are in reality identical with the 'I' of which I am aware? I do not know, and for the moment I shall not argue the point, since I can make judgments only about things which are known to me. I know that I exist; the question is, what is this 'I' that I know? If the 'I' is understood strictly as we have been taking it, then it is quite certain that knowledge of it does not depend on things of whose existence I am as yet unaware."[47] The adverb "precisely" indicates a limitation: for the ordering of knowledge, and only in the ordering of knowledge, thought is the necessary and sufficient condition in establishing the existence of one's self.[48]

47 *Meditations* in *The Philosophical Writings of Descartes, Volume II*, John Cottingham, *et al.*, II,18–19.
48 Cf. "Replies to the Fourth Set of Objections," in *The Philosophical Writings of Descartes, Volume II*, John Cottingham, *et al.*, 159. "Hence, had I not been looking for greater than ordinary certainty, I should have been content to have shown in the Second Meditation that the mind can be understood as a subsisting thing despite that fact that nothing belonging to the body is attributed to it, and that, conversely, the body can be understood as a subsisting thing despite the fact that nothing belonging to the mind is attributed to it. I should have added nothing more in order to demonstrate that there is a real distinction between the mind and the body, since we commonly judge that the order in which things are mutually related in our perception of them corresponds to the order in which they are related in actual reality. But one of the exaggerated doubts which I put forward in the First Meditation went so far as to make it possible for me to be certain of this very point (namely whether things do in reality correspond to our perception of them), so long as I was supposing myself to be ignorant of the author of my being. And this is why everything I wrote on the subject of God and truth in the Third, Fourth, and Fifth Meditations contributes to the conclusion

On this point Descartes undertakes a significant correction in the Preface with respect to what he already claims in the *Discourse* where he rushes to conclude the thinking nature of one's self directly from the *cogito*: "... it was not my intention to make those exclusions in an order corresponding to an actual truth of the matter ... but merely in an order corresponding to my own perception."[49] When divine truthfulness assures that clear and distinct ideas are true and thereby sanctions these results, we will be able to likewise assure that the nature of the mind consists only in thought and that none of the non-spiritual characteristics that the Aristotelian tradition attributes to the soul actually belong to it. "I shall, however, show below how it follows from the fact that I am aware of nothing else belonging to my essence, that nothing else does in fact belong to it."[50] Therefore, we can be sure, for example, that vital functions do not belong to the soul, which will be the pivot-point for the famous Cartesian theory even though it does not explicitly appear in the *Meditations* according to which animals would be without a soul insofar as their functions can be explained with the corporeal mechanism alone.[51]

2.3. *That the Mind Is More Easily Known than the Body*

The nature of one's self has been ascertained even in the absence of bodies, and even in the absence of its own body. The fact that knowledge of one's self, as an immaterial thinking substance, may be achieved independently of the knowledge of bodies is already enough to rip apart the empiricist's great premise that bodies are the first known thing (and so of all things best known) and that knowledge of the mind depends on it. Yet, it is

that there is a real distinction between the mind and the body, which I finally established in the Sixth Meditation."

49 "Preface to the Reader," in *The Philosophical Writings of Descartes, Volume II*. John Cottingham, *et al.*, 7.
50 Ibid.
51 Cf. *Discourse on the Method*, in *The Philosophical Writings of Descartes, Volume I*, John Cottingham, *et al.*, V, 134.

not enough to destroy the rooted popular prejudice (Aristotelian) according to which what one knows firstly and best are bodies, and where the faculties most relied upon are those of the senses and imagination. Following along the lines of this prejudice, the knowledge one has of the mind, or of that which in his being is not corporeal, is instead indirectly drawn from the act of knowledge of bodies. To definitively wipe that prejudice out, Descartes opts to bring it forward and sizes it up using its own terms. That is, Descartes wants to analyze the act of knowledge of bodies.

The Aristotelian reasons in this way: bodies are the first things we know; they are known through the senses; contact with the senses produces an image from which the intellect then extracts the intelligible species, which makes up the material for intellectual knowledge; the intellect, therefore, derives all its knowledge from the sense faculties. The intelligible species extracted from the image of the perceived object is, however, immaterial. One here deduces that the intellect that produces and hosts the intelligible species is also itself immaterial. The immateriality of the mind is inferred by the operations the mind puts into act in a pursuit of knowledge of bodies.

In this schema, the temporal ordering of knowledge also scandalizes the ordering of the greater or lesser ease and adequateness of knowledge itself. The body is better and more easily known than the mind because knowledge of the body precedes and is the condition for knowledge of the mind. The mind is less easily and less perfectly known inasmuch as knowledge of it depends on the act of knowledge of bodies. If the Scholastic had engaged in the imaginary Cartesian experiment, hypothesizing that bodies do not exist, he would have had to conclude that (in this hypothesis) the mind would not know anything, not even itself. Even Duns Scotus, who concedes the most to the possibility of intuiting the acts of the mind through simple introspection, follows Thomas Aquinas in saying that the essence of the mind, in its actual condition, is knowable only through abstraction from sensory knowledge. "In its actual condition, neither the soul nor our nature is known by us if not through some general concept abstracted through sensible things."[52]

Moving against this tradition, Descartes tries to show that knowledge of bodies depends on the nature of the mind: that which is immaterial is the condition for knowledge of that which is material. If he succeeds in his project, even Aristotelians (who think that the condition is better and more easily known than the thing conditioned) will have to admit that the mind is better and more easily known than bodies. In other words, if he succeeds, Descartes will accomplish an upheaval of the foundations of empiricism with its own terms. This is the first instance of direct confrontation with the arguments of his adversaries, and it is a confrontation driven by the pedagogical-persuasive agenda seen in the *Meditations*. The more the reader is led to break open the logic of his habitual reasoning and stir up results that might be contrary to what he normally came up with in the past, the more likely it is that he is convinced.

In the imaginary experiment concerning the knowledge of a piece of wax, Descartes one by one turns Aristotelian ideas on their heads. Every sort of knowledge of bodies (even confused and obscure knowledge) is made possible through the faculty that does not depend on bodies to exercise itself—the intellect. The characteristics perceived through the senses do not make up the true nature of a body. The true nature of a body is constituted by properties knowable through pure intellect alone. Pure thought, the essence of the mind, is known more easily and better than bodies. Through the experiment of the knowledge of wax, at the close of the meditations one sees that non-sensory knowledge is implied in all of our knowledge of the world and conditions it, and that clear and distinct knowledge of the external world never has its origin in the senses.

The experiment is introduced by a question that gives voice to a common belief, conquered but not convinced by the prior arguments on the nature of one's self. "But I cannot keep from

---

52   G. Duns Scotus, *Ordinatio,* Prol. Pars 1, qu. unica in I. *Duns Scotus: Opera omnia.* C. Balic, ed. Roma 1950. I, 17.

thinking that corporeal things, images of which are formed by means of my thought and fall under the senses might not be known more distinctly than what I do not know to be a part of myself, that does not fall under the imagination." The meditating self urges the old self, who is ready to return to the safety and refuge of his prejudices, to examine a piece of wax extracted from a beehive and take in through his senses all the splendor of its perceivable characteristics: its color, smell, hardiness, temperature, etc. Yet placed next to the fire all these characteristics are lost, and the wax heats up, liquefies, and loses its odor and color. Nonetheless the perceiving subject continues to judge the wax before him to be the *very same wax* as before. Hence, he is led to conclude that he sees a piece of wax but not on account of any of the previously realized qualities. So one must say that the conclusion "this is a piece of wax" does not depend on characteristics drawn through the senses.

One then tries to define wax as a body, or else as something "extended, flexible, and changeable." This time the definition of wax uses dispositional adjectives (flexible, changeable) that include both the current form of the wax as well as all of its future states. When I describe sugar as a soluble body, I have no problem admitting that sugar is the same body both when it appears in the form of dry crystals as when it is diluted in water. However, both the flexibility and mutability are not characteristics that one experiences by way of the senses. In fact, these senses can only produce perceptions limited to here and now. It is rather to the imagination that it seems to have recourse, at least in this case: I experience through my senses that wax is round, but through my imagination I conclude that it is capable of taking on other shapes, for example becoming square or rectangular. And so I define it to be a changeable body. I would then judge to have before my eyes the same wax when it is hard and cold or when it is warm and pliable. For from the very first moment that I perceived it, I knew by way of my imagination that this single body is capable of taking on many different shapes or forms.

But we judge that the wax, like any body, is subject to *infinite* change. The imagination can indeed attribute to the wax one shape after another, and to do so would need an infinite period of time to come up with the infinity of possible shapes which can be imposed on the wax. But the imagination is not capable of keeping up with this infinitude of possibility. It is not possible, then, to undertake this task of every possible transformation through the imagination, for if the imagination were the faculty by which I know what the wax is, I never would ever have defined it to be capable of taking on an infinite number of shapes. And yet it is precisely in this manner that I conceive of wax, as I conceive of any other body. Therefore, it is neither with the senses nor the imagination that I know bodies, rather with the intellect which is capable of expressing the infinite with a single concept, without the assistance of images. "The perception I have of [the wax] is a case not of vision or touch or imagination–nor has it ever been, despite previous appearances–but purely mental scrutiny; and this can be imperfect and confused, as it was before, or clear and distinct as it is now, depending on how carefully I concentrate on what the wax consists in."[53]

One may note that Descartes does not simply claim to have clear and distinct knowledge of wax when he defines it as an infinitely shapeable body, that is, when he knows it through his intellect; while he knows it by way of his senses, his idea of it is only obscure and confused. Descartes claims something even more demanding. The knowledge one has is made possible by pure intellect (*solus mentis inspectio*), always, even when there are sensible characteristics attributed to the wax. The alternative, then, is not between clear and distinct intellectual knowledge and confused and obscure sensory knowledge, rather between confused and obscure intellectual knowledge (when I attribute to the wax characteristics that one perceives through the senses) and clear and distinct intellectual knowledge (when I attribute to wax characteristics that I gather solely from the intellect). When I believe I

---

53 *Meditations* in *The Philosophical Writings of Descartes, Volume II,* John Cottingham, *et al.*, II, 21.

have a piece of wax, when I judge that this is the same piece of wax whether warm and pliable or cool and hard, in reality what I am doing is formulating a judgment that supersedes sensory data, and reveals the activity of the intellect. Does the reader need proof of this? Face the window and look out at the passers-by. You will not hesitate to say that you see human beings, yet all you are looking at are coats and hats that might as well be covering ghosts. Behold, you do not in fact see human beings, you only judge to be seeing them. Judgment always overrides sensory data and is precisely what makes sensory data possible. We believe we are seeing what we do not actually see with our own eyes on account of a judgment made by the intellect. Hence, none of the sensory characteristics authorizes me to say that a hard and cold body and a warm and pliable body are *the same* piece of wax. This judgment, then, does not depend on what I see and feel, rather, if anything, what I see and feel depends on the judgment. Aristotelian-Scholastic empiricism has thus been overturned using its own terms: much less does intellectual knowledge depend on experience than experience itself depends on intellectual knowledge (insofar as experience claims to be organized and not merely a kaleidoscope of sensation).

Refuting empiricism by bringing its positions to the fore is one central point of the attempt to undermine the empirical origin of mathematics and geometry. Much less does the intellectual triangle have its origin in the experience of triangular figures, as Descartes says to Gassendi, then the conviction of seeing triangles in irregular shapes that one meets with in sensory experience can be explained merely by theorizing that we compare those figures to the perfect triangle that we know intellectually. "Hence, when in our childhood we first happened to see a triangular figure drawn on paper, it cannot have been this figure that showed us how we should conceive of the true triangle studied by geometers, since the true triangle is contained in the figure…. But since the idea of the true triangle was already in us, and could be conceived by our mind more easily than the more composite figure of the triangle drawn on paper, when we saw the composite figure we did not apprehend the figure we saw, but rather the true triangle."[54] Sense experience is always a construction of the mind. The elements of this construction, as we shall see later on, are those ideas that are purely mental, that is, innate ideas such as the idea of the infinite extension and configurations that make possible judgments that *seem* to be of an empirical origin. For example, when I judged that I saw the same wax when I had a liquid or solid body in front of me. Innate Cartesian ideas, which in origin are purely intellectual, allow one to realize the components that lend structure to experience and make it possible, and that are in no way obtained through experience itself. Triangles haphazardly drawn by a child's hand are nonetheless recognized to be triangles. Fragmented data collected or experienced in various periods of time is organized as an experience of one single object. On the whole, each time we decipher a drawing and see human beings or trees in the lines sketched on a piece of paper, what we are doing is overcoming empirical data and organizing it into what we call "experience." Here Descartes opens up a way that, taken as far as it goes, leads one to Hume's position and then Kant who says that one must search one's own mind to find what makes experience possible, as this is all interwoven with elements not inferable from empirical data alone.

Experience is possible on account of ideas that do not come from experience. This first result immediately implies another: only when I know wax with the intellect and the intellect alone, that is as an extended body and subject to infinite configurations, do I finally have clear and distinct knowledge and know the nature of wax. For here I have reached the non-empirical notion that makes *all* knowledge of wax possible, even that knowledge presumed to be empirical. In what regards the wax, one is in reality now experimenting with an analysis of sensory experience already put into play in the doubt of the first meditation—the senses do not yield knowledge of the thing in itself. From sense

54 "Replies to the Fifth Set of Objections," in *The Philosophical Writings of Descartes, Volume II*, John Cottingham, *et al.*, 262.

perception it is necessary to go back and reference figures in the imagination, and then lastly to simple natures gathered and contained by the intellect and the intellect alone. Only the latter is clear and distinct knowledge, knowledge that cannot be analyzed further. If all knowledge is intellectual knowledge, it can be obscure and confused (when the contents of a judgment are based on material from the senses and the imagination) or else clear and distinct (when the content of a judgment derive from characteristics that I have no experience of but know instead through the intellect alone). One has clear and distinct knowledge of empirical data only when, digging into it from the inside, one traces back to those simple natures of mathematics that are never directly experienced. Nonetheless, they are implicit in every experience insofar as they are the condition itself for these experiences. In the direct experience of the decomposition of a body one thereby verifies that the very conditions of experience are found beyond, or apart from, the senses. Nevertheless, as is the case with the nature of the mind, for we do not know if what we know clearly and distinctly is true, we cannot yet say that mathematical characteristics really constitute the true essence of bodies. We can only say that the mind knows bodies by necessarily attributing to them those characteristics.

Now Descartes can achieve what he has been saying since the title of the meditation. Inasmuch as bodies are known through properties that do not come to us through abstraction from the bodies themselves, rather through ideas (of the intellect, pure thought, *a priori*), it follows that knowledge of the soul must be more easily acquired than knowledge of bodies. All of this is based on the principle that even empiricists admit, a principle according to which knowledge of a condition is easier to come by than knowledge of what is conditioned. "I see that without any effort I have now finally got back to where I wanted. I now know that even bodies are not strictly perceived by the senses or the faculty of imagination but by the intellect alone, and that this perception derives not from their being touched or seen but from their being understood; and in view of this I know plainly that I can achieve an easier and more evident perception of my own mind than of anything else."[55]

The analysis of the piece of wax is a confirmation of just how much Descartes means to show us through the argument of the *cogito*. In experiencing the wax I always refer back to the existence of my own self, at every level of knowledge that I have of it. Here one must not forget that the existence of the wax has been assumed at the expense of temporarily shattering our prior suspension of the existence of bodies. But it is always possible to reinstate the suspension, reviving the reasons that led to the doubt of the existence of bodies. So, firstly, the experiment of the wax demonstrates that *it seems to me* that I see wax, that *I think* I see it, and that I can doubt the existence of the wax but not that of my own self, the "I," that thinks it sees wax. Again, one notes that knowledge of the existence of one's self is implied in the *thought* of seeing wax, and so the experience of wax above all else reveals the nature of the mind (thought), and likewise its existence. The *cogito, sum* is here verified by concrete experience, and it is to the advantage of the further achievement of privileged access to the knowledge of the nature and existence of the mind with respect to knowledge of the nature of bodies.

2.4. Thought

Thought, as has been seen, constitutes the essence of one's self. But what is thought? What is the nature of thought? One arrives at thought by way of the negation of the existence of bodies, even one's own body, therefore thought is most assuredly immaterial. This is Descartes' main concern, and it is helpful to keep it in mind for it explains the oscillations as he determines the nature of thought throughout the course of the *Meditations*.

In a preliminary evaluation, the nature of the mind is described with the characteristics that various philosophical traditions have interpreted as incorporeal. "Therefore, to be precise, I

---

55 *Meditations* in *The Philosophical Writings of Descartes, Volume II*, John Cottingham, *et al.*, II, 22–23.

am nothing if not a thing that thinks, and that is to say a mind, an intellect, or a reason." More analytically, the nature of thought is described as a whole of the activities of thought. "But then what am I? A thinking thing, a thing that thinks. And what is a thing that thinks, a thinking thing? A thing that doubts, perceives, affirms, denies, wills, wills not, even imagines, and furthermore feels or senses." Among these activities of thought, some (such as conceiving) appear to be independent of the existence of bodies outside the mind. Hence they present themselves as most certainly immaterial. Other activities, such as imagining and feeling, seem to require the existence of bodies in order to exercise or project themselves. The specific relationship between bodies and the pure intellect on the one hand, and then between bodies and the imagination and senses on the other helps one understand why Descartes oscillates back and forth in determining the nature of thought. On the one hand Descartes favors the intellect, or the faculty that in no way relies on bodies for its content and to exercise itself. According to this line of thought, imagination and sense faculties do not make up the essence of thought. They are merely modifications of thought, so in the absence of the imagination and the senses, the nature of thought would simply remain the same. The reader sees this in the analysis of the piece of wax. "I now know that even bodies are not strictly perceived by the senses or the faculty of imagination but by the intellect alone, and that this perception derives not from their being touched or seen but from their being understood; and in view of this I know plainly that I can achieve an easier and more evident perception of my own mind than of anything else."[56] In the sixth meditation he returns to this point. "I consider that this power of imagining which is in me, differing as it does from the power of understanding, is not a necessary constituent of my own essence, that is, of the essence of my mind."[57]

---

56 *Meditations* in *The Philosophical Writings of Descartes, Volume II,* John Cottingham, *et al.,* II, 22–23.
57 Ibid., VI, 51.

Yet favoring pure intellection presents some difficulty, and it does not give itself easily to conceptualization. For example, it is not clear what the relationship between the imagination, sensibility, and the intellect might be. In the sixth meditation, Descartes attempts to think of this relation under the form of a modal relation. Here, the intellect represents the essence of thought while the imagination and sensibility are its accidents. "Besides this, I find in myself faculties for certain special modes of thinking, namely imagination and sensory perception. Now I can clearly and distinctly understand myself as a whole without these faculties; but I cannot, conversely, understand these faculties without me, that is, without an intellectual substance to inhere in. This is because there is an intellectual act included in their definition (...) I also recognize that there are other faculties (like those of changing position, of taking on various shapes, and so on) which, like sensory perception and imagination, cannot be understood apart from some substance for them to inhere in, and hence cannot exist without it."[58] It may be that here Descartes is referring to what he has already claimed in the second meditation—that is, sensing and imagining always imply pure understanding.

The second route, which runs alongside the first throughout the course of the entire *Meditations,* and which will stand out in the set of replies to the objections, is the decision to define thought with reference to the awareness that accompanies all its acts, independently of the fact that these may or may not imply the existence of external bodies. "It is also the same 'I' who has sensory perceptions, or is aware of bodily things as it were through the senses. For example, I am now seeing light, hearing a noise, feeling heat. But I am asleep, so all this is false. Yet I certainly *seem* to see, to hear, and to be warmed. This cannot be false; what is called 'having a sensory perception' is strictly just this, and in this restricted sense of the term it is simply thinking."[59] As we know, here "precise" indicates that something is considered

58 Ibid., VI, 54–55.
59 Ibid., II, 19.

independently from all else. And so the feeling or sense taken "precisely" means that that feeling is considered only insofar as it is an activity of the mind, that is insofar as one is aware that he is feeling or sensing something, and not in relation to the object (for this object could be non-existent). I am aware of all the acts of the mind and it is this awareness that constitutes the nature of thought. Being aware of willing, feeling, sensing, imagining, and all acts of the mind is the common denominator (immaterial, of course) in all activity of thought. Once defined in this way, thought, understanding, or conceiving no longer have the favored role with respect to feeling or sensing. Descartes makes this very clear in his *Reply to the Second Objections*. "I use [the term 'thought'] to include everything that is within us in such a way that we are immediately aware of it. Thus all the operations of the will, the intellect, the imagination and the senses are thoughts."[60] On the whole, awareness of the visual, audible, etc. is all that remains unattainable through doubt, even when the existence of each and every body is put into parenthesis. "It is possible that what I see is not really the wax; it is possible that I do not even have eyes with which to see anything. But when I see, or think I see (I am not here distinguishing the two) it is simply not possible that I am who am now thinking am not something."[61]

60 Ibid., "Replies to the Second Set of Objections," 160.
61 *Meditations* in *The Philosophical Writings of Descartes, Volume II*, John Cottingham, *et al.*, II, 22. Cf. *Principles of Philosophy*. I. § 9, 195. "By the term 'thought,' I understand everything which we are aware of as happening within us, in so far as we have awareness of it. Hence, *thinking* is to be identified here not merely with understanding, willing and imagining, but also with sensory awareness. For if I say, 'I am seeing, or I am walking, therefore I exist,' and take this as applying to vision or walking as bodily activities, then the conclusion is not absolutely certain. This is because, as often happens during sleep, it is possible for me to think I am seeing or walking, though my eyes are closed and I am not moving about; such thoughts might even be possible if I had no body at all. But if I take 'seeing' or 'walking' to apply to the actual sense or awareness of seeing or walking, then the conclusion is quite certain, since it

The anthropological foundations of the Cartesian theory of knowledge are set down in the second meditation. The mind is a substance independent of the body and so even the knowledge of what is material can be independent from experience. In emphasizing this independence of thought from corporeal faculties, Descartes chooses to call the content of thought *ideas* rather than intelligible species, as the Scholastics call the concepts formed by the human intellect starting from sensory images. Using the word "idea" Descartes wants to stress the autonomy of thought with respect to corporeal faculties. Indeed, the word "idea" was reserved by Thomas Aquinas for the content of divine thought. "I used the word 'idea' because it was the standard philosophical term used to refer to the forms of perception belonging to the divine mind, even though we recognize that God does not possess any corporeal imagination. And besides, there was not any more appropriate term at my disposal."[62]

3. Ideas and the Existence of God

The existence of the thinking self, the thinking "I," showed itself to be unobtainable by the doubt that revoked the belief in all other existence. Now one will have to take on the task of going back up from one's self to the taking back or recovery of the existence of the world. The third meditation opens with the hope of being able to use the characteristics of the first indubitable proposition *I think, I am* as the criteria that allows one to distinguish true propositions from dubious ones. The proposal is to judge as true all those propositions that have the same characteristics as the proposition *I think, I am*. The proposition *I think, I am* is "clear and distinct," therefore all propositions with analogous characteristics are equally true. "So I now seem to be able to lay

relates to the mind, which alone has the sensation or thought that it is seeing or walking."

62 "Replies to the Third Set of Objections," in *The Philosophical Writings of Descartes, Volume II*, John Cottingham, *et al.*, 127–128.

it down as a general rule that whatever I perceive very clearly and distinctly is true."[63]

Although by now the title "clear and distinct" given to ideas, and in general used for knowledge, is associated above all with Descartes, he did not actually invent it. Of the Scholastics Duns Scotus used it in a meaning similar to that of Descartes. Nonetheless, to avoid ambiguity, in his *Principles* Descartes thinks it necessary to define exactly what he means when he uses the phrase "clear and distinct" or "confused and obscure" with respect to ideas. "I call a perception 'clear' when it is present and accessible to the attentive mind (...) I call a perception 'distinct' if, as well as being clear, it is so sharply separated from all other perceptions that it contains within itself only what is clear."[64] Ideas can be clear without being distinct—one can clearly prove conscious pain and yet think that pain is something real in and of itself and in the part of the body that hurts, in this way attributing to the sensation of pain an objectivity that is not proper to it. But every distinct idea is necessarily also clear. An idea is rendered distinct when, through the effort of one's attention, only the characteristics truly and actually belonging to the object that the idea it represents are granted by attribution, and those that do not actually belong to it are eliminated. A good example of moving from an obscure idea to a distinct idea is when all the corporeal characteristics that are attributed spontaneously to the nature of the mind are one by one removed from it. For without these characteristics the mind continues to be conceived of as capable of subsisting. The idea of the mind is rendered clear and distinct when it is separated from all characteristics, without which it remains merely "the idea of my mind." In summary, that idea which represents the essence of a thing is distinct.

The sign that manifests the presence of clear and distinct

63 *Meditations* in *The Philosophical Writings of Descartes, Volume II*, John Cottingham, *et al.*, III, 24.
64 *Principles of Philosophy*, I, § 45, in *The Philosophical Writings of Descartes, Volume I*. John Cottingham, *et al.*, 207–208.

knowledge to the mind is the incapacity to doubt its truth. I can doubt the fact that I am walking, but not the fact that I am thinking. To say that all clear and distinct ideas are true means that, after the experience of the *cogito*, all knowledge that the mind is irresistibly brought to judge to be true would be declared to be true. Some propositions are so simple and so obvious that while they are under consideration they cannot be placed in doubt, for it is inconceivable that they might be false. For example, the finite mind is not capable of thinking that two plus three does not equal five. When I am faced with a proposition of this kind I cannot doubt it, in precisely the same way that I cannot doubt my own existence. Hence, by the force of the absolute truth of the *cogito* and the claim that doubt is inapplicable to some simple propositions, a hope emerges that one might be able to close the adventure of meditating and here on out declare as true all propositions that, like the *cogito*, are beyond doubt. Nonetheless, these propositions do not enjoy the same favor as does the existence of one's self. As we know, this is implicit in something that I can never be separated from—my own thought. This is why the *cogito* is confirmed by every thinkable reason for doubt, and not because it is a clear and distinct idea. On the contrary, I can detach myself from every other individual proposition and think of it under the general formula of "clear and distinct." When I think of them in this way I succeed in conceiving of a reason to place them in doubt. I can conceive of a God so powerful as to have created me in such a way that every time I consider a proposition that seems indubitable I deceive myself. In this situation I remain certain of existing, since my existence is the necessary condition for possible deception, and yet when I take it into consideration all the propositions that seem to be indubitable (like the *cogito*), when I attend to them, would appear as uncertain and dubious. The capacity of the mind to doubt, in an indirect manner, even those clear and distinct propositions that are the most simple, demonstrates that a reason for doubt still weighs on them. The threat of an infinitely powerful God evoked in the first meditation, the only thinkable reason (and not yet dealt with fully) for placing in doubt propositions that I cannot doubt as I consider them, is still in opposition to the use of the clarity and distinction of ideas as a sign of truthfulness.

> And whenever my preconceived belief in the supreme power of God comes to mind, I cannot but admit that it would be easy for him, if he so desired, to bring it about that I go wrong even in those matters which I think I see utterly clearly with my mind's eye. Yet when I turn to the things themselves which I think I perceive very clearly, I am so convinced by them that I spontaneously declare: let whoever can do so deceive me, he will never bring it about that I am nothing, so long as I continue to think I am something; or make it true at some future time that I have never existed, since it is now true that I exist; or [*vel forte etiam*] bring it about that two and three added together are more or less than five, or anything of this kind in which I see a manifest contradiction.[65]

With the "*vel forte etiam*," the Latin text softens the analogy between the impossibility on the part of the omnipotent God to enact deception regarding the propositions that adhere to the *cogito*, and the impossibility of ensuring that the mind deceives itself with regard to those propositions, albeit simple and indubitable, that adhere to mathematics, an analogy that the indubitable character of both would seem to justify.

There are two choices. Either one remains attached to the present, individual evidence and is content with its psychological indubitability, without even having the possibility of amassing its certainty of that of a later intuition. Or else one can attempt to demonstrate the truth of the general rule, "All things that we clearly and distinctly conceive of are true," and thereby eliminate the only reason for doubt that would keep one from subscribing

---

65 *Meditations* in *The Philosophical Writings of Descartes, Volume II*, John Cottingham, *et al.*, III, 25.

to it. In other words, one must demonstrate that God exists and is not a deceiver.

3.1. *The Nature of Ideas*

The only way to "achieve" the existence of some being other than one's self, while remaining faithful to the rules of meditating, is to utilize that which has already been acquired as truth, that is the existence of the thinking self and the content of thought—ideas. In fact, ideas can never be false because they precede the act of judgment. I can err in the judgment that things are as they are perceived, but I cannot err in the perceiving of them. "Now as far as ideas are concerned, provided they are considered solely in themselves and I do not refer them to anything else, they cannot strictly speaking be false; for whether it is a goat or a chimera that I am imagining, it is just as true that I imagine the former as the latter."[66] In the construction of the demonstration, the necessary axioms to accomplish it will be set right next to ideas, as these, too, are indubitable like the *cogito*. The axioms, in fact, are known by "natural light": "Whatever is revealed to me by natural light ... cannot in any way be open to doubt. This is because there cannot be another faculty both as trustworthy as natural light and also capable of showing me that such things are not true."[67] The reasons why axioms are not susceptible to falsity will be shown by Descartes by the fact that they are known through intuition and cannot be said to themselves be "science," rather only conditions of demonstrations and deductions, in which science properly resides. The axioms, and the *cogito,* which shares the characteristics of the axioms, are never susceptible to reasons for doubt. On the whole, even the reasons for doubt that can be thought of obey logical axioms—"because there cannot be another faculty ... capable of showing me that such things are not true." Therefore, like the *cogito,* any reason of doubt does not weaken them, rather confirms them.

66   Ibid., 26.
67   Ibid., 27.

Ideas, even before commencing the adventure of doubt, were the premise to inferring the existence of something outside the mind. Hence, ideas seem to have different origins. "Among my ideas, some appear to be innate [*innatae*], some to be adventitious [*advenitiae*], and others to have been invented by me [*factitiae*]. My understanding of what a thing is, what truth is, and what thought is, seems to derive simply from my own nature. But hearing a noise, as I do now, or seeing the sun, or feeling the fire, comes from things which are located outside me, or so I have hitherto judged. Lastly, sirens, hippogriffs and the like are my own invention."[68] Here Descartes introduces a division of ideas according to their origin that he elaborates on in the fifth and sixth meditations, but for the moment it is simply a division made in good sense and does not yet conclude anything with regard to the true origin of ideas. "But perhaps all my ideas may be thought of as adventitious, or they may all be innate, or all made up; for as yet I have not clearly perceived their true origin."[69]

Adventitious ideas are normally held to be the vehicle between thought and the external world. If I see the sun it means the sun exists. Yet, as we come to expect after the first meditation, the reasons which sustain spontaneous beliefs of the existence of the world on the basis of the presence of ideas in the mind (presumed to be of external origin) do not appear firm and beyond the reach of all doubt. An external world has to exist—one is inclined to believe—because adventitious ideas are involuntary. It is not I who decides to see the sun or not. But unbeknownst to myself I might possess a faculty that provokes these ideas, like what happens to us in dreaming. An external world has to exist because we are led to believe as much by a natural inclination. But inclinations are not clear and distinct ideas, and often in following them one chooses what is bad rather than what is good. Therefore they are not to be trusted in the pursuit of truth.

68   Ibid.
69   Ibid.

In sum, the route of the origin of ideas, which is followed spontaneously in the hope of gaining faith in the existence of a world and the likeness of this world to the ideas we have of it in our heads, can no longer be taken if one is attempting the demonstration of the existence of some being external to the self. Why is it not to be taken? On account of the doubt raised in the first meditation which has not yet been fully dealt with. Nonetheless, the possibility of coming to a true belief in the existence of other beings is through ideas alone, for insofar as they are modifications of thought only these are in my possession. We are talking about analyzing ideas from a different angle, no longer according to a presumed origin but instead according to their nature.

In what regards their nature, Descartes divides ideas into two categories—one is rather strict and the other a bit more broad. In the former, wherein ideas are considered strictly, properly speaking the name "idea" is given only to the mental events that represent something. In the latter category, every mental event, every act of thought, is an idea. "Some of my thoughts are as it were the images of things, and it is only in these cases that the term 'idea' is strictly appropriate—for example, when I think of a man, or a chimera, or the sky, or an angel, or God. Other thoughts have various additional forms: thus when I will, or am afraid, or affirm, or deny, there is always a particular thing which I take as the object of my thought, but my thought includes something more than the likeness of that thing. Some thoughts in this category are called volitions or emotions, while others care called judgments."[70]

In the first meaning, only mental events that have representative content are called ideas (ideas are always ideas *of* something). In the second meaning, even acts of thought such as wanting or judging are called ideas, that work on ideas in a strict sense and do not represent anything. The broadened notion becomes the favored notion of ideas as we see in Descartes' replies to

70   Ibid.

objections—everything I am aware of, acts of volition, representative states, and the judgments I formulate of those representative states are all called ideas. "I am taking the word 'idea' to refer to whatever is immediately perceived by the mind. For example, when I want something or am afraid of something, I simultaneously perceive that I want, or am afraid; and this is why I count volition and fear among my ideas."[71] In the *Meditations,* however, and most notably in the third meditation where the notion of idea is developed for the first time, the meaning of idea as a representative state is critical (ideas in the proper or strict sense), and necessarily so because the first proof of the existence of God in this meditation uses only this particular notion of ideas.

According to the lexicon inherited from the Scholastics, what an idea represents is called the *objective reality* of the idea. The objective reality indicates the type of reality due to a being for as much as it is the *object* of thought. For example, the lion considered in and of itself independently from a known thing or being has a *formal* reality. The same lion, insofar as it is actually known, has instead an *objective* reality inside the mind. Therefore, an idea in the proper sense is two-sided. On the one hand it is an act of thinking, and in this aspect all thoughts are equal. Here, the idea of God is, as an *idea,* no different than the idea of a man. On the other hand an idea represents something, has representative content, and because of this each idea is different from the next. The idea of a horse and the idea of a man do not differentiate themselves inasmuch as they are acts of thought, but insofar as they are each an idea *of* something, that they represent a horse and a man respectively, they are not the same and hence distinguished.

To understand these pages it is necessary to elaborate on another presupposition (whose theory does not appear until the fifth meditation) that plays an important role in the analysis of ideas. In a proper sense, all ideas represent something. Yet not everything that is represented is due some real or possible

---

71 "Replies to the Third Set of Objections," in *The Philosophical Writings of Descartes, Volume II.* John Cottingham, *et al.,* 127.

existence external to the mind. This is expected only of that representative content incorporated into real being. On this occasion Descartes is again indebted to the Scholastics. Real being includes only that which, having true essence, exists or, though not actually existing, can indeed exist outside the mind, like a rose in winter. The representative content that does not have an essence and thereby does not exist nor can exist outside the mind is not a part of real being. Here we are talking about, for example, contradictory beings like four-sided circles (the chimeras as Descartes calls them, again, like other Scholastics), fictional beings such as winged horses, or other entities of reason like negations and privations. The content of these have no reality in and of themselves. They are in and of themselves "pure nothing" and the only reality due them is that of simply being an object of thought. They exist as content of thought but they do not exist nor can they exist outside the mind. As objects of thought, a winged horse and a horse are never on the same level. Only the plain horse belongs to the sphere of real being because it can exist, its nature is "some thing," whereas a winged horse is *only* a thought. When we analyze innate ideas in the fifth meditation we see how Descartes puts himself to the task of establishing rigorous criteria as the basis for judging whether an idea represents a true essence or not.

Though not always representing something that belongs to real being, ideas in a proper sense always exhibit their representative content as if this content were due to a possible existence outside the mind. This, in fact, is the nature of ideas: "as ideas are like images, there cannot be an idea that does not seem to represent something." Once again, it is the Scholastic tradition that guides Cartesian theory. Being is the object of thought. It is not possible to think of nothing, and precisely on account of this fact the mind when it thinks of something that does not exist and cannot exist must think of it in the form of a real being, or else as if it were something. "Since the object proper to the intellect is being," says a Scholastic who Descartes knew well, Francisco Suarez, "it is not possible to conceive of nothing if not as a being, therefore when it tries to conceive of privation or negation, the intellect conceives of it as being, and thereby the entities of reason are formed."[72]

This theory allows Descartes to answer an objection that could be posed against his thesis that the qualities of objects do not have any objective reality outside the mind and are only subjective sentiments. One may observe colors, sounds, etc. represented as actually existing in objects and therefore seeming to be a part of real being. To this possible objection, Descartes responds with the theory of materially false ideas. It is a theory modeled off what Suarez uses to explain how negations and privations should be conceived of (as things that cannot exist outside the mind), and this permits Descartes to challenge the implication between being conceived of as not "pure nothing" and being that is actually "something," or that actually belongs to real being. There are ideas that represent something that in itself is not anything, what does not exist and cannot exist outside the mind. For the Scholastics this means negations and privations, and Descartes adds to this the sensible, or sensory, qualities of objects. But since the mind, in order to be able to think, always attributes at least possible existence to its content, sensible qualities (as well as negations and privations) are represented as if they were real. All the same, neither privations nor the qualities of objects can exist outside the mind, and so the ideas that represent them as bestowed with possible existence are intrinsically, materially false. In popular prejudice, which holds that the sensible (sensory) characteristics of bodies actually belong to the bodies themselves, there is a mechanism in motion that cannot be eliminated from thought, that thought is not possible but according to the notion of existence outside the mind that is at least possible.

Introducing the category of materially false ideas, Descartes seems to violate his own theory which states that ideas are neither true nor false and that truth and falsehood are found only in judgment. "Now as far as ideas are concerned, provided they are considered solely in themselves and I do not refer them to anything

---

72 F. Suarez. *Disputationes metaphysicae*, LIV, I, VIII.

else, they cannot strictly speaking be false (...) As for the will and emotions, here too one need not worry about falsity (...) Thus the only remaining thoughts where I must be on my guard against making a mistake are judgments."[73] On this point, with his objections Arnauld puts Descartes through the wringer. In answering him, Descartes tries to uphold the theory that renders ideas false, as well as the theory that marks truth and falsehood in judgments alone. Materially false ideas are those obscure and confused ideas that lead one to maintain that what is represented in an idea can exist outside of that very same idea, which leads one to make a false judgment.

The notion of the material falsehood of an idea is what we utilize when we call jewelry false. False jewelry is, for example, something that claims to be gold, so much so that one forms a false judgment after examining it. Properly speaking, it is not the jewelry that is false, rather the judgment I make of it. Yet, the jewelry has been crafted in such a way as to bring about that false judgment, and for this I label it false. The perceptions of the mind that do not have a representative content due to the possibility of it existing outside the mind are made in such a way as to lead one instead to believe that what they represent might exist, since every idea by nature attributes possible existence outside the mind to the thought-up thing. This is why Descartes can add that the material falseness of an idea consists in its leading one to false judgments. As the jewelry has been thus crafted so as to make one believe it were gold, and hence lead one to a false judgment, so obscure and confused ideas are made in such a way as to lead one to judge that they represent something that exists or can exist beyond the thought of it. But it is not so. When the obscure and confused ideas that represent qualities of objects through careful observation are made to be clear and distinct, their representative content becomes a sentiment of the subject. And sentiments, or feelings, do not exist outside the mind. Red ceases to be a characteristic of flowers in order to appear as what it actually is,

73 *Meditations* in *The Philosophical Writings of Descartes, Volume II,* John Cottingham, *et al.,* III, 26.

a modification by the mind. Yet next to the clear and distinct idea, there remains the illusion of seeing colors as if they were in the objects, and so materially false ideas are perpetuated. Clear and distinct ideas of corporeal things replicate but do not eliminate obscure and confused ideas of a sensation. But they keep the mind from incurring a false judgment.

In contrast, all those clear and distinct ideas that represent beings that exist, or can exist, outside the mind are materially true, and their objective reality is constituted by beings that are part of real being. Favorite examples of these ideas are the ideas of the essences of mathematics, due to the fact of the possible existence, and the idea of God, which in turn is due to a necessary existence. Descartes proposes the following three-fold schema: clear and distinct ideas = true ideas = ideas that represent something that has reality, is real. The fact that the representative content of some ideas belongs to real being justifies the presupposition on which, as we will soon see, the first proof of the existence of God is supported. According to this proof there must be a cause for the objective reality of ideas, for everything that has reality, everything that is real, has a cause.

The notion of materially false and materially true ideas is very important in the undertaking of the meditative way. Inasmuch as true ideas of essences represent "something," like everything that is real, these must depend on God. Membership of true ideas to real being, then, is one of the reasons why God is called on to guarantee them (the other reason is the incoercibility of the assent that the mind gives them).

3.2. *The Existence of God and the First* a posteriori *Proof*

Descartes has three worked-out proofs for the existence of God. Two of these are *a posteriori* proofs wherein he begins with effects and traces their cause. The third, an *a priori* proof, comes in later in the fifth meditation. In all three it is quite evident that the idea of God plays a central role, and each proof is constructed using elements of the theory of ideas that we have just dealt with.

The first *a posteriori* proof begins with an analysis of ideas in their proper sense. Insofar as both are acts of thought, the idea of a horse and the idea of a man are not different from each other. But they are differentiated in the fact that one represents a horse, and the other a man. The representative content of ideas can be structured around the grade of reality that such content represents. The grade of reality is established on the basis of the autonomy of the being represented. The idea of a finite substance represents a being that does not need anything but God to subsist and therefore has greater objective reality than ideas which represent accidents, which rely on substance to exist. The idea of infinite substance is the idea of being that only needs itself in order to subsist and therefore has greater objective reality than the idea that represents a finite substance insofar as the finite substance requires infinite substance in order to subsist. Descartes adds to this analysis a principle made manifest "by way of natural light," an axiom, then, on the basis of which "there must be at least as much [reality] in the cause as in the effect."[74] Descartes presents the principle of causality as a fundamental axiom, so much so that he deduces from it the principle "from nothing, nothing comes." A being can be produced by a cause that has the same reality as its effect (*formal* cause) or that has greater reality than its effect (*eminent* cause). But that which has lesser reality cannot produce something that has greater reality.

The meditator realizes that he must preliminarily ascertain for himself that the elements that he will employ in the proof of the existence of God not only invoke the inclination to assent (something that could turn out to be deceitful), but further characteristics that are able to ensure that no prejudice is insinuated in any part of the proof. Essentially, "the longer and more carefully I examine all these points, the more clearly and distinctly I recognize their *truth*."[75] Thereby armed with an effect that cannot be false like an idea and a necessarily true axiom, like the principle of

---

74 *Meditations* in The Philosophical Writings of Descartes, Volume II, John Cottingham, *et al.*, III, 34.
75 Ibid., 29. Emphasis mine.

causation, the meditator can sketch a proof of the existence of God firmly formed solely of clear and distinct ideas, to assent to which (if it is convincing) the mind will have been led by "natural light" alone and not some "inclination" that is not justifiable by reason.

The principle of causality applies to both the formal and objective reality of ideas. An idea, considered as a simple modification of thought, cannot account for the diversity of its representations. Consequently, one will have to look beyond ideas and among those beings bestowed with formal reality for the cause responsible for the fact that one idea represents a man and another a horse. So, through the principle of causality one is compelled to say that the representative content of all ideas comes from some cause that contains in itself at least as much reality as is contained in the idea of it. At the height of the third meditation the meditator sees one single being bestowed with formal reality—the thinking substance. The self, insofar as it is a finite thinking substance, has enough reality to be the formal cause of ideas of other finite substances. Indeed, it has greater reality than clear and distinct ideas of the modes and accidents of those substances, for example, the geometrical-mathematical properties of corporeal substances. The self could be the formal cause of the clear and distinct ideas of finite substances, and eminent cause of the clear and distinct ideas of accidents. Even more so, the thinking self even has enough reality to produce confused and obscure ideas. In fact, on account of their obscurity and confusion, it is difficult to determine if what these ideas represent belongs to real being or not. That is, if these represent something that can exist outside the mind. For all one knows of the matter, confused and obscure ideas could really be materially false, and what is therein represented not be a part of real being. In this case the representative content would not require a positive cause. To explain its origin would be a matter of invoking the imperfection of the subject and nothing more. If the representative content had belonged to real being, their confusion and obscurity would attest to the fact that the reality due them must be so meager as to be produced by one's self, a finite substance.

Only one idea has greater objective reality than formal reality contained in one's self. Here we are dealing with an idea of infinite substance, of God, an idea that cannot therefore be produced by one's self. It follows that an infinite substance capable of causing in me the idea of the infinite must exist, and exist outside of my thought.

The Cartesian proof can be mapped out like this:

There must at least be as much reality in the cause as in the effect.

The cause of the objective reality of ideas must have at least the same formal reality as objective reality contained in the idea.

The thinking self possesses the idea of an infinite substance.

The thinking self, inasmuch as it is a finite substance, does not have enough formal reality to cause the objective reality of an infinite substance.

Therefore, there exists an infinite substance that has caused the objective reality of the idea of infinite substance.

In light of this deduction one might raise the point that one's own self might very well be the cause of the idea of God, inasmuch as the idea of the infinite might be obtained through negation of finitude. That is, the idea of the infinite could be a negative idea, and a finite being would thereby be capable of producing it. This objection that Descartes advances is really the Aristotelian-Scholastic conception of the knowledge the human mind can have of the infinite. That is, the finite intellect cannot have positive knowledge of the infinite. The idea of the infinite is a negative notion that one comes by through negation, and precisely the negation of the limits of what is finite. It is the idea of the finite, if anything that is a positive and primary notion, and from this the notion of the infinite is derived. If this concept of the knowledge that the human mind has of the infinite were correct, Descartes' proof would not be sustainable insofar as even the idea of the infinite would have to be produced by one's finite self and hence there would be no proof of the existence of God. Descartes is well aware of this and is ready to assert the necessary condition to maintain his proof: the finite intellect has a positive and primary idea of both God and the infinite.

In order to maintain the legitimacy of considering the idea of the infinite positive and primary, Descartes does not hesitate to take a hammer to Scholastic arguments. For to Descartes it is not the idea of the infinite that derives from the finite, rather the idea of the finite that derives from the infinite. The linguistic form of *in*finite and finite is messy—it presents a notion that in reality is positive and primary as negative and derived, and the negative and derived notion to be positive and primary. One's self could not perceive himself as doubting, and thereby imperfect, if he had not compared himself to a being that is entirely perfect. The idea of the infinite is a primary idea and is already implied in the idea of the doubting self.

This also excludes the hypothesis that the idea of God is a materially false idea, that what it represents is not actually part of real being. Contrary to the theory that the idea of God is materially false, the theory of "true" ideas returns to the fore. In contesting that the idea of God is not materially false, Descartes asserts the clearness and distinctness of the idea of the infinite. Because it is clear and distinct, the idea of God represents something that belongs to real being, and therefore it must be a "true" idea. And not only this—the representative content of the idea of God has *more* objective reality than any other clear and distinct idea and this makes it the truest idea of all, the most real. The gradation of the amount of objective reality possessed by ideas allows for the gradation of the truth of ideas. "[This idea] is utterly clear and distinct, and contains in itself more objective reality than any other idea; hence there is no idea which is in itself truer or less liable to be suspected of falsehood. This idea of a supremely perfect and infinite being is, I say, true in the highest degree (...) [this idea] is the truest and most clear and distinct of all my ideas."[76]

This statement is anything but banal. It brings to its apex the

76 *Meditations* in *The Philosophical Writings of Descartes, Volume II*, John Cottingham, *et al.*, III, 32.

Cartesian claim of the positive knowledge of the essence of God, a knowledge that until Descartes no one had claimed so definitively. The rupture is particularly evident when one compares Descartes with Thomas Aquinas. In the latter, man cannot answer the question "What is God?" but only speak about what God is not. Human knowledge of God is always negative and imperfect knowledge.[77] Indeed, even according to Aquinas, it is impossible to know God (and the infinite) by way of ideas, which are always finite. As he says, "No created species is sufficient to represent the divine essence."[78] Descartes is aware of the audacity of his theory, and formulates two arguments in its defense. In the first place, the idea of God *is* clear and distinct, even clearer and more distinct than any other idea for all that is known as perfect in a clear and distinct way is attributed to God. Therefore God, inasmuch as he is most perfect, is the source of all clear and distinct ideas. The second argument is more sophisticated. As happens with the negative interpretation of knowledge of the infinite, Descartes utilizes the strongest objections against his position to construct his own argument. Here he does so for the clear and distinct idea of God. Those who maintain that the human mind cannot have a clear and distinct idea of God pivot on the incomprehensibility of God. As Gassendi remarks in his objections, "But first of all, the human intellect is not capable of conceiving of infinity, and hence it neither has nor can contemplate any idea representing an infinite thing (...) God is infinitely beyond anything we can grasp (...) Hence we have no basis for claiming that we have any authentic idea which represents God."[79] Affirming that the human mind has a clear and distinct idea of God, Descartes also has to support the position that claims man has access to the essence of God, that God is comprehensible to the human mind, which appears to be an unprecedent presumption.

77 Thomas Aquinas, *Summa Theologiae*, I, 3.
78 Thomas Aquinas, *De veritate*,10, art.11.
79 "Replies to the Fifth Set of Objections," in *The Philosophical Writings of Descartes, Volume II*, John Cottingham, *et al.*, 200–201.

Descartes' answer to this objection consists of, first of all, the defense of his position with regard to the incomprehensibility of God, and in the denial that such incomprehensibility undermines the clearness and distinctness of the idea of God. The nature of the infinite implies that it is incomprehensible to the finite mind. Therefore, he who claims to comprehend the infinite admits in the same breath to *not* have a clear and distinct idea of it, since he would believe himself to be thinking of the infinite, but in reality he is only thinking of the finite, which indeed is all that the finite and hence limited human mind can grasp. Only he who does not comprehend the infinite can maintain that he possesses a true, and therefore clear and distinct, idea of its nature. "This idea is, moreover, utterly clear and distinct (...) It does not matter that I do not grasp the infinite (...) for it is in the nature of the infinite not to be grasped by a finite being like myself. *It is enough that I understand the infinite* (...) This is enough to make the idea that I have of God the truest and most clear and distinct of all my ideas."[80] To avoid equivocations on this point, Descartes provides a further precision of terms. In what regards God, one can never use the notion of "comprehension." The verb "to comprehend" with its implicit metaphor alludes to the possibility of enclosure in the mind, of knowing something adequately.[81] When dealing with God, we instead use the verb "to understand," meaning that we know with certainty that God is infinite, yet we do not and cannot adequately know all the properties of an infinite entity. "For the idea of the infinite, if it is to be a true idea, cannot be grasped at all (...) Nonetheless, it is evident that the idea which we have of the infinite does not merely represent one part of it, but really does represent the infinite in its entirety (...) so it suffices for the possession of a true and complete idea of the infinite in its entirety if

80 *Meditations* in *The Philosophical Writings of Descartes, Volume II,* John Cottingham, *et al.*, III, 32. Emphasis mine.
81 Cf. Descartes to Mersenne, 27 May 1630. *AT* I, 152. "To understand, this is to embrace thought. But to know a thing, it is sufficient to touch on it with thought." Cf. *K,* 15.

we understand that it is a thing which is bounded by no limits."[82]

The incomprehensibility of God, in this case, is the result of true knowledge (clear and distinct) of his infinity. And thus Descartes answers Gassendi who accuses him of having a heretical position regarding the comprehension of the infinite. ["With respect to the idea of the infinite which] you say cannot be a true idea unless I grasp the infinite (....) My point is that, on the contrary, if I can grasp something, it would be a total contradiction for that which I grasp to be infinite. For the idea of the infinite, *if it is to be a true idea, cannot be grasped at all*, since the impossibility of being grasped is contained in the formal definition of the infinite."[83] The involvement between true knowledge and the incomprehensibility of God *places in opposition* the strong Cartesian cry of the impossibility of comprehending the infinite against all forms of Agnosticism or negative theology. It is because one "understands" truthfully the infinite nature of God that one cannot comprehend it.

In the end, one cannot say that the idea of the infinite could be obtained through the progressive increase of my own perfections. In such a case the idea of God would be the idea of infinitude *in potency*, while the clear and distinct idea of God represents it as *actually* infinite.

82 "Replies to the First Set of Objections," in *The Philosophical Writings of Descartes, Volume II*, John Cottingham, *et al.*, 253–254.

83 "Replies to the Fifth Set of Objections," in *The Philosophical Writings of Descartes, Volume II*, John Cottingham, *et al.*, 253. Emphasis mine. See also, 252: "Here you fail to distinguish between, on the one hand, an understanding which is suited to the scale of our intellect (and each of us knows his own experience quite well that he has this sort of understanding of the infinite) and, on the other hand, a fully adequate conception of things (and no one has this sort of conception either of the infinite or of anything else, however small it may be)." Cf. Descartes' letter to Mersenne, 28 January 1641. *AT* III, 293. "I have never written about the infinite if not to subject myself to it." Cf. *K*, 93.

3.3. *The Existence of God. The Second* A Posteriori *Proof.*

Descartes judges the proof of the existence of God deduced from the cause of his idea of God (for he will always be disposed to it) to be quite evident—and it will always be his favorite proof of the existence of God— even though it is easily obscured as soon as attention to it is abated. This hinges on almost completely innovative reasoning, indeed on the necessity of finding the cause of the content of ideas. The novelty of the argument contributes to the difficulty of keeping the momentum of the persuasion that Descartes means to produce in the course of the demonstration. That is why he proposes a second *a posteriori* proof (or reformulation of the first), which is probably more familiar to the reader. Here, instead of searching for the cause of an idea, he looks for the cause of the being, the only being that, at this stage in the *Meditations,* might bestow existence—that is, he is looking for the cause of his thinking self. In this way, the *a posteriori* proof comes as close as possible to the model of one of the most famous *a posteriori* proofs of the existence of God—the causal proof delineated by Thomas Aquinas as the second way of demonstrating the existence of God.[84] It looks like this:

> In the world, every being must have a cause.
> In the search for a cause one cannot pursue it unto the infinite degree.
> Therefore, there exists a first uncaused cause, and that is God.

In the Thomistic proof, the point of departure is the finite being existing in the world. On this model Descartes attempts to demonstrate that God exists beginning with the only finite being of which he can know the existence: his own self.

This is the second time after the passage about the piece of wax that Descartes engages attentively in the models of proofs set down by the Scholastics. He is renewed in his faithfulness to the require-

84 Thomas Aquinas, *Summa Theologiae,* I, 2, ad 3.

ments of meditation and sowing the seeds of his new philosophy in the field of tradition. But at every step of his proof, Descartes introduces such significant modifications that what ends up happening is a radical disfiguration of what Thomas Aquinas laid down. The first novelty is that even in this proof the idea of God is present, and as we shall see it plays a very important role. It is not simply about finding the cause of one's self, rather it is dealing with the cause of *one's self in possession of the idea of God*. One is no longer in the infinite searching for the cause, as in the first proof, rather in the realm of the finite—though only insofar as one possesses in himself the idea of the infinite. The premise sounds like this: in possession of the idea of God, one's self must have a cause.

In the first place, Descartes considers the theory of he himself being the cause of his own existence something to discard immediately, for he who has given himself being would have also given himself every perfection that he can think of. But one's self does not have all the perfections that he can think of, and so he has not given himself being. The capacity to give oneself all the perfections in he who has given himself his own being is justified by the reason that one's self is a substance and perfections are, instead, modes of substance. Therefore, he who has enough power to give himself being, to create substance or something that has more reality than the attributes, will also have what it takes to create the attributes of that same substance. However, this reasoning is missing something, for he who has enough force to give himself the attributes proper to substance could also *not* want to give them to himself, to *not* exercise his full capacity. In such a situation, the imperfection of one's self could not exclude the capacity to give oneself being. Descartes takes a strike at this empty argument in the *Reply to the Second Objections,* adding the missing premise: the will always bears itself unto the good it clearly knows.[85] Therefore, if one had the capacity to give himself every perfection he can think of, he would certainly have done so. But one experiences his

---

85   Cf. "Replies to the Second Set of Objections," in *The Philosophical Writings of Descartes, Volume II,* John Cottingham, *et al.,* 117.

own self to be imperfect and so he cannot be the author of his own being.

This first passage, apart from introducing the innovative presence of the idea of God in the Thomistic schema, hides a truly surprising novelty with respect to tradition. Descartes shuns the idea of self-causality, just because one does not have all the perfections that he has the idea of. This means that Descartes does not judge the hypothesis that a being is its own cause necessarily contradictory in and of itself. This theory of self-causality was, however, in and of itself considered contradictory by the Scholastics. "It is not possible that someone be the efficient cause of himself because he would have to be prior to himself, and this is not possible,"[86] says Thomas Aquinas, and no one would have contradicted him on this point. If a Scholastic would have been the author of the proof Descartes proposes, he would have concluded, "Seeing as no being can cause itself, the self cannot give itself being."

Self-causality done away with, Descartes considers the theory that one's self has no cause, that one's self is eternal. But this theory excludes the necessity of a cause in the past, but it does not exclude the necessity of a cause in the present. For Descartes, it is evident to anyone who considers the nature of the life span of a finite entity. The permanence in existence of a finite entity can be interrupted at any moment, which means that what happens in one moment of time has no relation to what happens in the next. "For a lifespan can be divided into countless parts, each completely independent of the others, so that it does not follow from the fact that I existed a little while ago that I must exist now, unless there is some cause which as it were creates me afresh at this moment—that is, preserves me."[87] From this premise, Descartes

"The will of a thinking thing is drawn voluntarily and freely (...) but nevertheless inevitably, towards a clearly known good. Hence, if it knows of perfections which it lacks, it will straightaway give itself these perfections, if they are in its power. Whatever can bring about a greater or more difficult things can also bring about a lesser thing."

86 Thomas Aquinas, *ST* I, 2, ad 3.

comes to an extremist interpretation of the Scholastic theory that holds that a constant intervention by the first cause is necessary to preserve and conserve creatures in being. To be kept in existence, in fact, is interpreted as continuous creation. To explain the existence of a being in the present, one necessarily presumes that there be a cause that has the power to create, a cause that exercises the very power "that would be necessary to produce or create something all over again, as if it had not yet come to be." I do not possess such a power, which if I had would always be in act because I gave myself being, and so I would be aware of exercising it. One's self must, therefore, have a cause that is not itself.

This cause could be some being less perfect than God. Yet the principle of causality calls for a search of a cause that has at least as much reality as is contained in its effect, and the effect in question here is one's self, the thinking substance in possession of the idea of God. Hence, the cause that conserves one's self in the present must be a thinking substance that possesses the idea of all divine perfections. This cause either exists through itself or it exists through something else. If it exists through itself it has to have given itself all the perfections of which it has an idea. This is based on the reason behind the exclusion of self-causality in the case of one's self, which again pivots on the point that he who has enough power to give himself being also has the power to give himself all the perfections that he can think of. If it exists through something else, one has to search for the cause in a being that has either given itself being or obtained it from something else. Here one risks triggering an infinite regression wherein one only and always comes to a being caused by another being. Now, an infinite regress with regard to causes would be inevitable if one searches for the cause that has acted in the past and that now might no longer exist. In this case, the infinite regression is cut out in that one is instead searching for the cause that acts in present time. "It is clear enough that an infinite regress is impossible here,

87 *Meditations* in *The Philosophical Writings of Descartes, Volume II,* John Cottingham, *et al.*, III, 33.

especially since I am dealing not just with the cause that produced me in the past, but also and most importantly with the cause that preserves me at the present moment."[88] The second premise of the Thomistic proof (infinite regression of causes is impossible) is transformed by Descartes into the following: *In the present* an infinite regression of causes is impossible.

One has to go as far as to a final cause that is not caused by anything else, hence caused by itself, and so contains in itself all the perfections of which it has the idea. This is God. In the case of one's self this kind of causality is left out, but it is how one justifies the jump from being *per se* to something having in itself every perfection. In order to leave out self-causality of the self one might say, "Seeing as it does not have all of the perfections of which it has the idea, the self could not have given itself being." Instead, now one concludes: "Seeing as the first cause is the cause of its own being, it will have all the perfections of which is has an idea, and this is God." The Thomistic conclusion, that there exists a first uncaused cause, this is God, is transformed by Descartes into, "There exists a first cause that is *the cause of itself,* and this is God."

Caterus is the first to take notice of the fact that the Cartesian *a posteriori* proof requires a notion that is rejected as contradictory by Scholastics—the notion of self-causality. He provides Descartes with the possibility of a relentless defense, a defense repeated again after the offensive of the fourth objector, Antoine Arnauld, on this same point. Like all the theologians before him, Descartes maintains that God, as opposed to finite beings caused *by something else,* or by other beings, is a being *per se.* But the Scholastics reject self-causality as contradictory, and thereby have interpreted the notion of being *per se* to be a *negative* notion: God is *per se* in the sense that he has *no cause,* that he does *not* depend on something else. Descartes on the other hand interprets this same notion to be positive. The Cartesian God exists *per se,* in the sense that he is the cause of himself and, precisely, *causa sui.* According to Descartes this notion ceases to appear contradictory

88   Ibid., 34.

if only one does not mean to take the cause of one's self literally as the *efficient* cause of one's own existence. The causality that God exercises with respect to his own existence is instead a *formal* causality. Understood in this way, the causality through which God produced his own existence can be translated into more familiar terms—the essence of God is cause of his own existence in the sense that it is the *reason* that God exists, in the way the nature of the triangle is the reason for the equality of each of the three angles in a equilateral triangle.[89] The innovative extension of the causality of God becomes an axiom in the appendix to the *Reply to the Second Objections* in the discussion of metaphysics the "geometric way." "There is not anything in existence that one cannot ask the cause for its existence." Because one attributes a cause to every existing thing, what is not caused by something else cannot but be caused by itself. To the Scholastic claim of something either being caused by something else or not caused, Descartes holds up the alternative of something being caused by something else or caused by itself, in light of the principle of the universality of the principle of causality.

The justification Descartes provides for his inference of the existence of a being *causa sui* gives rise to some perplexity. A being that is the cause of itself has to exist, because an infinite regression is impossible in the present moment. In the first place, Cartesian physics foresees the infinite division of the finite, and so even if the present moment in which one searches for the cause is finite, it is unclear why the infinite regression has to be left out. Secondly, even

89 "Replies to the Fourth Set of Objections," in *The Philosophical Writings of Descartes, Volume II,* John Cottingham, *et al.,* 167. "What derives its existence 'from another' will be taken to derive its existence from that thing as an efficient cause, while that derives its existence 'from itself' will be taken to derive its existence 'from itself' will be taken to derive its existence from itself as a formal cause(…) I think it is necessary to show that, in between 'efficient cause' in the strict sense and 'no cause at all,' there is a third possibility, namely 'the positive essence of a thing,' to which the concept of an efficient cause can be extended."

if one conceded that in the present moment an infinite regress is not possible, this circumstance would constitute a good argument in favor of the existence of a final cause, but would not provide any argument to support the notion that the final cause is also the cause of itself. Essentially, the inference, which is not at all convincing, of a cause of itself from the impossibility of infinite regression in the present moment is flanked in the *Reply to the First Objections* by the theory that states that the cause that has enough power to sustain a being in being must also have sufficient power to give being to itself. Therefore, from the simple fact that there must be a cause of the existence of the self in present time, one infers that the cause of that bestows being on the self is *causa sui,* and that it will have therefore given itself all the perfections of which it has an idea. This new argument does not only eliminate every reference to the impossibility of infinite regression, it also excludes the possibility that there are more than one causes that conserve the self in present time: the single existence of a being that does not have sufficient power to create itself and therefore to conserve itself implies the existence of a being that does, in fact, have sufficient power to create a substance, also has enough power to cause its own existence.[90]

In summary, this is the schema of the second *a posterior* proof:

90 "Replies to the First Set of Objections," in *The Philosophical Writings of Descartes, Volume II,* John Cottingham, *et al.,* 80. "And each one of us may ask himself whether he derives his existence from himself which suffices to preserve him even for one moment of time, he will be right to conclude that he derives his existence from another being, and indeed that this other being derives its existence from itself (there is no possibility of an infinite regress here, since the question concerns the present, not the past or the future). Indeed, I will now add something which I have not put down in writing before, namely that the cause we arrive at cannot merely be a secondary cause; for a cause which possesses such great power that it can preserve something situated outside itself must, *a fortiori,* preserve itself by its own power, and hence derive its existence *from itself.*" Emphasis mine.

1. The future existence of something does not follow from the present existence of that thing.

2. In every moment an existing being continues in its existence, there is a necessary cause of this continually recreated existence (because of proposition 1).

3. The cause of a being must possess all the reality possessed by that being either formally or eminently.

4. There exists a being in possession of the idea of God, one's self, a finite thinking substance.

5. The cause of one's self in possession of the idea of God must be a thinking substance in possession of the idea of God (because of 3 and 4).

6. The cause of one's self is, or has being, either per se or through something else.

7. If the cause of one's self is through something else other than itself, it is caused by another thinking substance in possession of the idea of God (because of 3).

8. Infinite regression is not possible in present time.

[In the *Reply to the First Objections,* propositions 6, 7, and 8 are substituted with: He who has enough power to give being to another substance has enough power to give being to himself.]

9. There exists a first cause of one's self that is, or has being, per se (because of 6, 7, and 8).

10. He who has enough force to give himself being has enough power to give himself every perfection that he has an idea of.

[In the *Reply to the Second Objections* the following premise is inserted: He who knows what is good and has enough power to procure it, will indeed move himself to procure it.]

11. The first cause has enough force to give itself every perfection (because of 9 and 10).

12. The first cause has the idea of every perfection (because of 5).

13. The first cause necessarily gives itself every perfection that it has the idea of (because of 10, 11, and 12).

14. Therefore, the first cause is a most perfect being, and this is God.

Certainly there is a bit of grandeur in this proof with respect to the first *a posteriori* argument, as well as the *a priori* proof of the fifth meditation. And with respect to its model, Thomas Aquinas' causal proof, it is extraordinarily complicated.

So much complex argumentation in Descartes can be explained by his intention to reproduce the Thomistic schema familiar to readers, though introducing correction in the places he thinks are defective. If we try to reproduce the Cartesian proof according to the Thomistic schema, Descartes' corrections (and violations) hit the reader smack in the face.

They are these corrections, these violations, that help us understand the critique Descartes issues Aquinas and the novelty of his theology. He is explicit on this latter point with Caterus.

Thomas Aquinas	Descartes
In the world every being must have a cause.	One's self *in possession of the idea of God* must have a cause.
(Aquinas denies that one can have the idea of God.)	
One cannot proceed to an infinite degree in the search for a cause.	*In the present moment* one cannot proceed to the infinite.
(Descartes attributes erroneously to Aquinas the search of a cause in the past)	
Therefore, a first uncaused cause exists.	Therefore, a first *cause, which is the cause of itself,* exists.
(For Aquinas, self-causality is impossible.)	

The first correction, even in this proof, is the insertion of the idea of God. Under provocation from Caterus, Descartes clarifies the irreplaceable function the idea of God plays in his *a posteriori* proofs ("all the force of my demonstration depends on that alone"). Essentially, "it is this same idea which shows me not just that I have a cause, but that this cause contains every perfection, and hence that it is God."[91] Descartes' critique of Aquinas is clear: without knowledge of God, knowledge that Thomas Aquinas rejects as impossible in the human mind, it is not possible to prove that the first cause is God. If one simply looked for the cause of one's self, one would not succeed in proving that the first cause is a most perfect being. The idea of God in both *a posteriori* proofs of his existence is irrevocable. "It matters little that my second demonstration, founded on one's own existence, might be considered to be different from the first, or as some kind of explanation for it (...) Yet it seems to me that all these demonstrations, obtained through the effects, boil down to one—that even these are imperfect if these effects are not evident (...) and if we do not center the idea that we have of God in this. Because (...) even if one arrives at a first cause that conserves me, I cannot say that it is God if I do not truly have an idea of God."[92]

While still engaging Caterus, Descartes explains why he chooses to go forward with his proof searching for the cause of the existence of his own self in the present rather than adhere to the Thomistic causal proof, which in his opinion goes back in the regression of causes in the past. For Descartes the Scholastic is wrong in claiming that a first cause can be discovered in this way. Thomas Aquinas is also guilty of this. According to Descartes, Aquinas holds that infinite regression of causes in the past is impossible inasmuch as it is incomprehensible. But the fact that infinite regression, as everything that has to do with the infinite, is incomprehensible, does not in any way imply for Descartes that in

91 "Replies to the First Set of Objections," in *The Philosophical Writings of Descartes, Volume II,* John Cottingham, *et al.,* 78.
92 Descartes to Mesland, 2 May 1644. *AT IV,* 112. Cf. *K,* 147.

itself it is impossible. If Descartes had done as he supposed Thomas Aquinas had done, and searched for the first cause going backwards in a series of causes in the past, he would have gone on infinitely never happening upon a first cause. On the contrary, in searching for the cause that acts in present time there is no risk of infinite regression. The search in the present for a cause that conserves a being whose origin is in question is therefore due to the necessity of creating particular conditions that inhibit infinite regression. Here, too, there is in this innovation a radical criticism of the Thomistic proof. Actually, Descartes is wrong on this point. Aquinas never looked for a cause of existing things in the past, rather for a cause whose actual action is necessary for the present existence of something. So, Aquinas already expressed his causal *a posteriori* proof in a search for the actual cause of the existence of something, supposing that only in these circumstances is the infinite regression of causes not possible. In fact, if the causes acting in the present were infinite, it would follow from an actual infinity, and for Aristotle and his followers an actual infinity is impossible. In this matter the difficulty is very much on Descartes' side. For Descartes the search for a cause in the present cannot eliminate the regression *in infinitum*, for he admits the possibility of an actual infinity and, following Cartesian physics, infinite division is always possible, even in finite space or time. Consequently it is the Cartesian rather than the Thomistic causal proof that is incapable of getting rid of the regression *in infinitum* and of arriving at a first cause in present time. This arduous problem is resolved in the *Reply to the First Objections*, where, as we have seen, Descartes eliminates exactly the question of the regression in search for the causes that conserve the self in present time, affirming that for the conservation of an existing being only one cause is required.

In the end, Descartes defends the legitimacy of the notion of *causa sui* to Caterus. With Arnauld he goes back to it, simply clarifying that the only way to demonstrate that the first cause of finite effects is God is to introduce the notion of self-causality. For, he says, if the only interpretation of being *per se* was the negative one, that is saying merely that it does not depend on anything else, this "would eliminate the means by which one can demonstrate the existence of God by the effects."[93] The notion of self-causality and the possession of the idea of God are the two conditions that make possible the demonstration that the first cause is also a most perfect being. This is founded on the argument that states that he who has enough power to give himself being (that is, he who is *causa sui*) has enough power to give himself all the perfections which he has an idea of. If he has the idea of every perfection, this being is God.

To find a first cause it is necessary that one modify Thomas Aquinas and incorporate an attempt to find the conserving cause of the present moment. To demonstrate that this cause is an infinitely perfect being, that it is God, one cannot bypass introducing the idea of God and the notion of *causa sui*.

The whole of these replies to objections helps us understand the decision-making process for choices made in the Cartesian *a posteriori* proofs. Even when he tries to reply to the framework of Thomistic proofs, Descartes' proofs distance themselves farther and farther from the Thomistic model on account of devastating, though meaningful, assumptions. Descartes' intention to confront and resolve the problem surrounding the passage from some finite reality, even of one's self, to the infinite and infinitely perfect reality, or the reality of God, is the reason for his insistence on the necessity of including the idea of God and the notion of *causa sui* in his proofs. The difficulty of this passage is something Descartes deems unresolved in Thomistic theology. Descartes maintains that all of the theology that begins a proof of the existence of God with some finite effect will never demonstrate that the cause of that effect is infinite. How can one infer the infinite from the finite, the infinitely perfect from the imperfect? Descartes eludes this difficulty. His first proof does this by assuming as its point of departure an infinite effect—the objective reality of the idea of God. The

93 "Replies to the First Set of Objections," in *The Philosophical Writings of Descartes, Volume II,* John Cottingham, *et al.*

second proof does so by starting with a finite effect, one's own self, and with the help of the notion of *causa sui* and the presence of the idea of God overcomes this initial disadvantage (the first cause, having produced itself, will have had to give itself all the perfections that it has the idea of and so is infinitely perfect).

Thanks to the clear and distinct idea of God, that God exists is demonstrated. That same idea assures us that God cannot be a deceiver, "since it is manifest by the natural light that all fraud and deception depend on some defect."[94] The proof of divine truthfulness, necessary in order to free the mind from doubt of the truth of clear and distinct ideas, is found once the "*vetus opinio*" of a most potent God is transformed through the effort of attention into a clear and distinct idea. We know that God, because of his infinite potency, has the capacity to see to it that the mind accepts false evidence of something, but that he will never use that power. For if he did so, the human mind would be drawn into deception by God himself and this is impossible insofar as other than being infinitely powerful, he is also truthful. In reality, divine truthfulness is nothing other than a consequence of God's being infinitely potent, for deception reveals weakness. "And although the ability to deceive appears to be an indication of cleverness or power, the will to deceive is undoubtedly evidence of malice or weakness, and so cannot apply to God."[95]

3.4. *The Idea of God*

The two *a posteriori* proofs that have as their central point the idea of God are not pressed for the origin of this idea. In his conclusion, Descartes briefly acknowledges this point when he simply says that the idea of God is innate. In the spontaneous division of ideas that opens the third meditation, only the faculties of thought are cited as examples of innate ideas. "My understanding of what a thing is, what truth is, and what thought is, seems to derive

94 *Meditations*, in *The Philosophical Writings of Descartes, Volume II*, John Cottingham, *et al.*, III, 35.
95 Ibid., 37.

simply from my own nature."[96] By way of the idea of God, we know there are in our minds some innate ideas "in the proper sense," or ideas representative of something that correspond to possible or truly existing beings outside the mind.

It is by excluding other possible origins that the origin of the idea of God is obtained. The idea of God cannot simply be an adventitious idea, because contrary to what occurs in instances of adventitious ideas that come up spontaneously in the mind, the idea of God requires a voluntary decision to grant its attention. The idea of God cannot be made up, for the content of this idea imposes itself on the mind without the possibility of manipulating or modifying it, as happens in cases of made-up ideas that are the handiwork of the thinking subject. "The only remaining alternative is that it is innate in me, just as the idea of myself is innate in me."[97] Yet even here Descartes does not offer a full theory of inneism, but we already know how to recognize an idea as innate from a made-up or adventitious idea.

There is a peculiar significance to the fact that the idea of God is innate. It is innate because it is the individual himself who bears the imprint of his creator, and so instead of saying that one *has* the idea of God one can say that one's self *is* the idea of God. "Of course, one ought not think it strange that God, in creating me, has placed this idea in me, like the mark a laborer leaves on his own work. And neither is it necessary that this mark be something different from the work itself." As of a painting that bears in itself the manifestations and traces of its author, I can say that this is *a* Caravaggio, *a* Bellini, likewise I can say of my own nature that it is the very idea of God inasmuch as it bears likeness to God.

Descartes' theory that states that I bear the image of God takes up again and emphasizes that which, already widely diffused, states that creatures manifest their divine origin through some likeness to the creator. In the fourth meditation, Descartes singles out the will (infinite in man as it is in God) as the faculty that

96 Ibid., 26.
97 Ibid., 35.

bears the image of God the most. In the analysis of the idea of God that comes at the end of the third meditation, however, Descartes insists on an aspect that we are already aware of—finitude is only intelligible through a comparison with infinitude, and so if I know myself to be finite it is only because I compare myself to the perfections that I do not possess yet have an idea of. The very clear and distinct idea of finite nature implies and is made possible by knowledge of the infinitely perfect. "But precisely thinking through what God created me it is rather believable that he has in some way produced me in his image and likeness, and that I recognize this resemblance (in which one finds the idea of God contained) by means of the same faculty through which I conceive of myself. That is, when I reflect on myself, not only do I know that I am an imperfect thing, incomplete and dependent on something else, something that tirelessly aspires for something better and greater that I am not but know of all the same, and of which I have ideas." I can have knowledge concerning my finite nature because I have knowledge of the infinitely perfect. We are not talking about tracing the infinite from the finite, as happens in all theology that distinguishes marks of the divine in human nature, rather understanding what is finite thanks to the knowledge of the infinite inscribed in the finite mind.

On the one hand, the analysis of the idea of God confirms the precedence of clear and distinct knowledge of the infinite over that of the finite. On the other hand, it recovers the idea of absolute perfection through an analysis of finite nature. Insisting on the knowledge of God through a created idea in the Cartesian project comes across as a rejection of the Thomistic position which holds that God cannot be truthfully known through a created idea in that nothing finite can adequately represent the infinite. "It is impossible (...) that the divine substance is seen through something created. (...) It is impossible that the divine essence is known by way of a created image."[98] It is precisely this violation, that the idea of God "is born and produced in me," all the more insisted upon as Descartes asserts the implication of the idea of the infinite in the clear and distinct knowledge of finite nature, that gives a stoutness to the Cartesian project in guaranteeing science without contact with the divine. The human mind has no direct contact with the divine but it does have clear and distinct knowledge of the divine nature discovered as internal to finiteness. Again, knowledge of God does not imply any direct relation to the divine nature, nor any supernatural insight. The guarantee of clear and distinct ideas has been discovered in another clear and distinct idea, inscribed in the finite nature of one's very self.

4. Error

Now that the idea of God has been made clear and distinct, the task of demonstrating the existence of God is accomplished, and we are furthermore certain of his truthfulness. In this sense, one can say that *a priori* we are certain of divine truthfulness. Yet there remains an objection to deal with, and if it is not resolved one risks invalidating the entire Cartesian deduction. If God is truthful, how is it possible that man falls into error? Divine truthfulness would seem to imply that man cannot ever be deceived, yet error is a daily experience. To establish the divine truthfulness once and for all, as well as guarantee clear and distinct ideas, Descartes has to demonstrate the compatibility of divine truthfulness and the experience of error. This comes to us in the fourth meditation. Essentially, Descartes gives notice in the synopsis of the *Meditations* that only with the fourth meditation can the initiative to establish clear and distinct ideas call itself complete. As he says, "In the Fourth Meditation it is proved that everything that we clearly and distinctly perceive is true..."[99] Only in the fourth meditation is divine truthfulness definitively demonstrated, for in this meditation the objection against divine truthfulness beginning with error is resolved. Otherwise, if it is not resolved, all that which has been argued up to this point will be rendered invalid.

98   Thomas Aquinas, *Summa contra gentiles,* III, cap. XLIX.
99   "Synopsis," in *The Philosophical Writings of Descartes, Volume II.* John Cottingham, *et al.,* 11.

4.1. God and Error

From the perspective of truth and error, Descartes here reproduces the classic theological problem of divine responsibility with regard to evil. If God is good, where does evil come from? Descartes tweaks the eternal question: if God is truthful, where does error come from? In the case of moral evil the effort of theology goes to demonstrating that the evil present in the world is compatible with the reality of divine goodness. For philosophers engaged in the metaphysical foundation of science, the task is to demonstrate that the experience of error does not authorize one to question the divine truthfulness just established as perfection in God, nor to continue to doubt clear and distinct ideas.

In order to overcome this latter obstacle to the guarantee of clear and distinct ideas, Descartes maps out the schema of the theodicy found in the Augustinian-Thomistic tradition. This theodicy distinguishes two kinds of evil: the evil of negation and the evil of privation. The first indicates the constitutive limit of a determined nature. If fish cannot fly, it is not for this that something of its nature is missing, that therefore the Creator owes something to the fish. The fish is perfect in its species even without wings, and this type of deprivation is merely a consequence of the finiteness of every creature. Hence, this does not imply any responsibility on the part of God, and thereby it is improper to call it evil. The second indicates, instead, the absence of something that is a part of a particular nature (the lack of sight in a human being, for example). Herein lies the real problem of theodicy. For one supposes that God himself has established human nature in such a way that it must have the gift of sight, and that therefore the absence of it is objectively a defect or error, and that this absence cannot be according to divine design. The evil of privation *par excellence* is moral evil, sin, the evil that deprives a creature of a perfection which it seems to be destined to have from the creator. It is above all from this evil that theodicy tries to exonerate God.

In the Augustinian-Thomistic tradition, this is done through two basic theories. In the first place, with respect to God, every evil is always reducible to an evil of negation. Finite beings necessarily lack something, though this something is not proper to their natures, and it is not due beings by nature. Nevertheless, the very finiteness of the human creature implies the possibility to verify what seems to be a real evil of privation. This is the case with moral evil, which deprives the human being of some perfection proper to its nature. With respect to God, evil refers back to the finiteness of creatures and the fallibility of the free human will, or the limits intrinsic to and constitutive of human nature, which have been instituted by God in the beginning. For man, however, it is still an evil of privation, for it depends on a free choice carried out in violation of a divine precept (what men know they must do). Since the choice could have been different and the evil was avoidable, the human being is responsible for it. Evil, then, has no positive reality with respect to God. Therefore, God is not the cause of evil nor can he *a fortiori* be judged responsible for it. "With the term evil there is indicated a particular absence of the good."[100] Nonetheless, the justification of God does not in any way implicate the absolution of men who are left alone to bear the full responsibility of sin. Men, in fact, would have been able to avoid staining themselves with sin through a better use of freedom. This argument pivots on free human choice. God created human nature to be fallible in its finiteness, though not condemned to evil because mankind is free in its exercise.

When one understands that God thought to create a perfect work and yet sin renders this work imperfect, one asks why God has not impeded man from doing evil in their free will. In his response to this question, his second argument sustains that the presence of evil contributes to the beauty of the whole, as shading might add depth and beauty to a painting. Hence, this world is better with evil in it than without it. "Many good things would vanish if God had not permitted there to be evil."[101] In this way, the presence of evil is made to be compatible with the supposed

---

100 Thomas Aquinas, *Summa theologiae*, I, 48, *ad*1.

divine project of creating a perfect work, or God's divine goodness, when it contributes to the perfection of everything (speaking here from the infinite perspective of God). Evil, then, does not limit divine goodness and perfection, nor does it stand in the way of divine objectives. On the contrary, the divine design utilizes the presence of evil in the world to realize its ends.

The arguments Descartes takes up to justify God in the face of accusations of God's responsibility when it comes to human error are structured along these lines. Error is on the one hand presented as a by-product of finitude, and on the other hand a result of the bad use of free will. Furthermore, God allows man to fall into error because error contributes to the overall perfection of his work.

4.2. *The Theory of Judgment*

Following the Augustinian-Thomistic schema of theodicy, Descartes proceeds to restore error to an evil of negation with respect to God, though for man it is still an evil of privation. A theory already delineated in the third meditation states that error is present only in judgment, and so in searching for the key to the origin and responsibility of error one has to begin here. So in the first place, one has to demonstrate that all the faculties involved in judgment, and all those faculties that man has received from God, make a human being perfect in his nature. Secondly, one needs to demonstrate that the error that occurs through the exercise of these faculties is due entirely to the bad use of free will.

According to Descartes, two faculties are involved in making judgments: the intellect and the will. The intellect contains the material of the judgment, the ideas and their relations, whereas the will manages the true and proper judgment in the assenting, dissenting, or abstaining from giving consent. Therefore, each of these faculties is to be pressed further in order to verify whether or not it harbors an evil of privation that God might be responsible for. Or better still: the human intellect is finite, but not imperfect by nature in its species, nor does one see why God has deemed

101 Ibid.

to bestow upon a finite creature a intellect broader than itself. The will, in turn, is not limited, and precisely in its indefiniteness the will is that which in man bears the image of the infinite and of God. "It is only the will, or freedom of choice, which I experience within me to be so great that the idea of any greater faculty is beyond my grasp; so much so that it is above all in virtue of the will that I understand myself to bear in some way the image and likeness of God."[102] The identical extension of the will in man and God is demonstrated by Descartes with an argument that he seems to deduce from the fact of the identical nature of the human and divine will. "[The will] does not seem to me to be (...) greater [in God than in man] if one considers it formally and very carefully in one's self," and independently from the other faculties. For in God these other faculties would be infinite, granting the divine will an effectiveness and firmness that man will never know in himself. The nature of the will is not susceptible to being more or less—it is the same in any subject that has a will. "This is because the will *simply consists* in our ability to do or not do something ... or rather, it consists simply in the fact that when the intellect puts something forward for affirmation or denial or for pursuit or avoidance, our inclinations are such that we do not feel we are determined by any external force."[103]

Yet a justification of this type places itself in open conflict with the theory of free creation of eternal truths, that Descartes was expounding on in a parallel text to the one at press, through his letter exchanges; of course, even if the theory in this parallel project plays no role in the *Meditations,* one can reasonably presume that Descartes never intended to defend a text that openly contradicted it and thereby would have rendered it unrealizable. According to the theory of the free creation of eternal truths, God is indifferent with respect to good and evil, because he would have been able to establish other criteria for truth and goodness, while

---

102 *Meditations* in *The Philosophical Writings of Descartes, Volume II,* John Cottingham, *et al.,* IV, 40.
103 Ibid. Emphasis mine.

the human mind cannot but consent to those propositions whose opposite implies contradiction, and cannot but recognize as good that which God had desired to be good. One's bearing before the true and the good is crucial in establishing whether or not the human and divine will are univocal, and it is evident that if the theory of the free creation of eternal truths is true, they bear themselves in a way that is completely deformed—opposite of what Descartes seems to be now saying.

Mersenne, hidden behind the anonymous identity of the authors of the *Sixth Objections*, forces Descartes to rethink the justification he gives in the fourth meditation in his claim that the human will is infinite. The author of the sixth objections notes that if the essences of things are indivisible Descartes would have also had to deny that indifference is part of the nature of divine will, for Descartes in his work says that indifference is not part of the essence of the human will.[104] Descartes replies, nothing can be predicated of God and man with the same exact meaning. "The fact that the essences of things are said to be indivisible is not relevant here. For, firstly, no essence can belong univocally to both God and his creatures."[105] Descartes here returns to his point of

---

104 Cf. "Replies to the Sixth Set of Objections," in *The Philosophical Writings of Descartes, Volume II,* John Cottingham, *et al.,* 219. Gassendi's objection in the fifth collection of objections is also relevant. "You say that you recognize your will to be equal to that of God—not, indeed, in respect of its extent, but essentially. But surely the same could be said of the intellect, too, since you have defined the essential notion of the intellect in just the same way as you have defined the will." In sum, in order to demonstrate the infinite nature of the will starting from its essence presents a two-fold difficulty. In the first place, no essence, not even that of the intellect, includes in its definition a reference to its extension. Therefore if the sharing of the definition with divine faculties had been enough to judge the human will to be infinite, even the human intellect would have to be judged infinite and equal to the divine intellect. In the second place, this would open up the way towards a sharing of nature for humans and God in an open contrast to the genuine spirit of Cartesian theology.

the doctrine of the divine will with respect to the good and the true, and explicitly theorizes it after having already done so publicly in his reply to Gassendi. "As for the freedom of the will, the way in which it exists in God is quite different form the way in which it exists in us. It is self-contradictory to suppose that the will of God was not indifferent from eternity with respect to everything which has happened or will ever happen; for it is impossible to imagine that anything is thought of in the divine intellect as good or true, or worthy of belief or action or omission, prior to the decision of the will making it so."[106] This answer closes off the way for the possibility of inferring the infinitude of the human will from the singularity of the essence of human and divine will. In the *Principles,* Descartes drops every attempt to justify the likeness between the human and divine will beginning with the nature of the will, and limits himself to the analogy between the extension of the human will (potentially infinite), and the extension of the divine will. "The will, on the other hand, can in a certain sense be called infinite, since we observe without exception that its scope extends to anything that can possibly be an object of any other will—even the immeasurable will of God."[107]

In any event, the two faculties involved in judgment, the intellect and the will, are not lacking anything. So there is no error of defect attributable to God. Nevertheless, error is a fact, and it is generated through the disproportion of the faculties involved in judgment. The inequality among the intellect (finite) and the will (infinite) is revealed in the phenomenon of error and explains why error occurs. When the material offered by the intellect is obscure and confused, the will can go beyond what is provided and affirm something from that content. That is, it might judge something to be true or false despite the fact that there might be various

105 "Replies to the Sixth Set of Objections," in *The Philosophical Writings of Descartes, Volume II,* John Cottingham, *et al.,* 292.
106 Ibid., 291.
107 *Principles of Philosophy* in *The Philosophical Writings of Descartes, Volume I,* John Cottingham, *et al.,* I, 35, 204.

elements lacking to carry out such an affirmation. This capacity to override the data of the intellect has been exploited by the doubt of the first meditation, in declaring false those things that are probable but not yet evident. There is only one instance where the will cannot withhold its assent—when one finds himself standing before a clear and distinct idea. In this case, judgment remains voluntary, even if there is only ever one result. In sum, according to Descartes judgment is always a voluntary operation and insofar as it is voluntary it is always free. In the case of obscure and confused ideas, the freedom of judgment is a freedom of indifference. The mind can affirm, deny, and suspend judgment. But in the case of clear and distinct ideas, the freedom of the judging subject consists in not being determined by other things while formulating one's assent, which in this case one cannot avoid. The will "consists in our ability to do or not do something (...) or rather, it consists simply in the fact that when the intellect puts something forward for affirmation or denial or for pursuit or avoidance, our inclinations are such that we do not feel we are determined by any external force. In order to be free, there is no need for me to be inclined both ways; on the contrary, the more I incline in one direction— either because I clearly understand that reasons of truth and goodness point that way, or because of a divinely produced disposition of my inmost thoughts—the freer is my choice. Neither divine grace nor natural knowledge ever diminishes my freedom; on the contrary, they increase and strengthen it."[108] Precisely because it is tied to the possibility of error, Descartes here gives his reductive judgment of the freedom of indifference. For him it is the lowest degree of freedom inasmuch as it is always accompanied by incomplete knowledge. "But the indifference I feel when there is no reason pushing me in one direction rather than another is the lowest grade of freedom; it is evidence not of any perfection of freedom, but rather of a defect in knowledge or a kind of negation."[109]

108 *Meditations* in *The Philosophical Writings of Descartes, Volume II,* John Cottingham, *et al.,* IV, 40.

In the thesis that Descartes means to maintain in this passage, it is crucial that judgment be voluntary. In this way one is always responsible for his own errors. With respect to mankind, error remains morally reprehensible, hence punishable, inasmuch as it is a free violation of a moral command that God has stamped in the human mind and which obliges him not to assent to anything but in the event that that assent is compulsory. That is, in the situation where one is standing before clear and distinct ideas. It is actually quite probable that Descartes elaborated his theory of the willfulness of judgment at the very end of constructing his justification of God through human error, and in full analogy to the traditional justification of God in the face of the presence of evil in the world. In the *Regulae ad directionem ingenii,* judgment is considered to be work of the intellect alone. The summons implicating the will in the genesis of error here permits Descartes to rest the entirety of responsibility on free human choice. On the flip side, the decision to pay attention to or take into consideration what is true and thereby render error impossible has positive moral value in Descartes. In fact, it adheres to a precept inscribed on the human mind by God, according to which "it is clear by the natural light that the perception of the intellect should always precede the determination of the will."[110] Divine commandment compels man to pursue the conditions where the choice between consenting and denying is no longer an issue, no longer possible. The moral value that Descartes attributes to the pursuit of truth clarifies all the more how the project of dedicating spiritual exercises, "meditations," to the search for what is true is anything but a gimmick of literary style.

The first step in justifying God passing along the route traveled by Augustinian-Thomistic theodicy has been taken: error, with respect to God, is a simple negation in that it is on account of the fact that one of the two faculties involved in judgment, the intellect, is not infinite and God was not forced to bestow on man a greater, wider intellect. Error, therefore, does not require *positive*

109 Ibid.
110 Ibid., 41.

causality on the part of God. Men, on the other hand, are entirely to blame for the errors they make because in falling into error one freely chooses to violate a moral commandment stamped on his or her own mind, a precept that keeps one from issuing a judgment unless he or she is standing in front of a clear and distinct idea. God was not compelled to grant man a greater intellect, while men are compelled to make better use of their free will, maintaining a will within the limits of the intellect.

4.3. Freedom

The page dedicated to an analysis of freedom and the will, which according to Descartes coincide (*voluntas sive arbitrii libertas*), contains two definitions of the will. "It consists only in this: that we can do something or not do it (that is, affirm or deny, pursue or abandon). Or rather only in this: that in order to affirm or deny, follow or flee from what the intellect proposes, we act in such a way that we do not feel pressured by any outside force." Faced with the freedom of the will, philosophers have always been divided into two principal schools of thought. There are those thinkers who tend to identify freedom with the voluntary nature of acts. This is generally held by determinists. Any and all action is free provided that it is not accomplished under duress. All voluntary actions are univocally determined, yet totally free. In this way freedom and necessity are linked. On the other hand, the non-determinists hold that not every voluntary action is free, only those that result from a free choice. One is not free when one is univocally determined to want or will something (for example, love towards one's children, or in many philosophers even love for the greatest good), but only when the choice could have been otherwise. Freedom, in this case, is present only in a subset of voluntary acts. There is a sense in which even the non-determinist can say that he is free even when he is univocally determined in his choice. One is free in front of the greatest good, though he cannot do otherwise but pursue it. One is actually *more* free in the face of the greatest good as opposed to the situations of choice between more imperfect things, for in dealing with greater goods one better realizes the ends of human nature, and releases it from the snares of imperfection. But in this case the non-Determinist will, in a certain sense, slip up in his use of the notion of freedom and move from a psychological meaning of freedom to a moral meaning. Descartes does something similar in his two-fold definition of freedom.

Reasoning with the logic of a non-Determinist, Descartes makes the distinction between actions that might have been different and actions univocally determined. But he maintains that in both cases the will is free, and actually *more* free in the case of necessary, voluntary consent. There is no doubt that Descartes in his theory of knowledge has a need for the capacity to suspend one's consent when faced with what is obscure and confused (error is always avoidable), as well as the impossibility to deny one's consent once, through the exertion of the attention, the mind has been directed towards those ideas which are clear and distinct. Again, compulsory consent is actually an unmistakable sign that the mind finds itself in front of something true. The creaturely character of the human will consists in this, that finding what is true to be already established by God the will necessarily grants its consent, as opposed to the divine will which is the free designer of what is true and thereby indifferent to it. But Descartes refuses to accept that in these cases judgment although voluntary is not free and even pinpoints the essence of freedom in the necessity of consent. "Thus the supreme indifference to be found in God is the supreme indication of his omnipotence. But as for man, since he finds that the nature of all goodness and truth is already determined by God, and his will cannot tend towards anything else, it is evident that he will embrace what is good and true all the more willingly, and hence more freely, in proportion as he sees it more clearly. He is never indifferent except when he does not know which of the two alternatives is the better or truer, or at least when he does not see this clearly enough to rule out any possibility of doubt."[111]

Descartes' decision to simultaneously claim that man partakes of the freedom of indifference but that herein one does not find the essence of freedom is due to a detour from the psychological notion of the freedom of the will to a moral notion. This detour can be explained through the desire to defend and uphold the worthiness and merit of assenting to the truth, hence a concern of assuring not only the voluntary nature of this assent, but also the freedom.

Yet this is not Descartes' last word on the subject. In later years, there were letters dedicated to the theme of freedom wherein he accentuates the role of freedom in the choices of the will and carves out a space for its exercise even in the act of adhesion to the truth. The will is not indifferent when faced with the good and the true, yet man can choose to disregard the truth or distract himself so as not to create the conditions that call for necessary assent. It is always possible to distract oneself from the truth clearly known and, in this case, assent is not necessarily given.[112] Descartes, then, prefers to call the power of choice, always present in the will, a "real and positive potency to realize itself." He reserves the title "indifference" for the condition of uncertainty that comes with weak knowledge of something. In doing so, at least verbally, he does not contradict all that which is laid out in the fourth meditation. That is, then, so as not to contradict the claim that the essence of freedom does not consist in indifference. In this version, indifference does not determine the field of play for the exercise of freedom of choice. The will can always choose differently, not only when it is indifferent, even misinformed, in the matter in question upon which it is called on to make a judgment. That emphasizes even more the merit and worth of one's consent to the truth. In fact, consent to the truth is necessary only once the will, in its power to realize itself, remains in full attention. On the whole, the possibility of doubt with regard to clear and distinct ideas is entrusted to the able employment of attention, as one reads the beginning of the third meditation.

111 "Replies to Sixth Set of Objections," in *The Philosophical Writings of Descartes, Volume II,* John Cottingham, *et al.,* 292.
112 Cf. Descartes to Mesland, 2 May 1644. *AT* IV, 115–16. Cf. *K,* 147. Emphasis mine.

In the text of the fourth meditation, Descartes does not simply confirm that we are free when we are not "compelled by exterior force." Rather, we are free when "we *do not feel we are moved* by any external force."[113] Right away he clarifies that he means to make a claim for the compatibility of freedom with predestination and grace. "The more I incline towards in one direction—either because I clearly understand that reasons of truth and goodness point the way, *or because of a divinely produced disposition of my inmost thoughts*—the freer is my choice."[114] Pressed on this thorny issue, Descartes never allows himself to get derailed from the conviction that the acts of the will are always determined by God, reapplying the limits of the human intellect in order to understand how this might reconcile itself to the freedom of the will.[115] Nonetheless, such a decisive admission read in these pages of the fact that the absence of determination that we experience in ourselves is nothing more than a *feeling* will be fodder for the determinists and contribute to the undermining of one of the traditional proofs of the freedom of the will, the proof derived from the feeling internal to one's own autonomy. Spinoza likens this proof to what happens in a stone as it does not feel determined by anything during its fall to the bottom of a pit.[116]

The necessity of assent when faced with clear and distinct ideas sheds light on one of the reasons (together with the membership of "true" ideas in real being) by which Descartes is able to invoke the guarantee of divine truthfulness. In fact, God would be a deceiver if clear and distinct ideas were not true, because it is not possible to withhold one's consent. In this case, there is no way to go about correcting an eventual error. It is this irreversibility of a belief that legitimizes the call for a truthfulness of the Being who

113 *Meditations* in *The Philosophical Writings of Descartes*, John Cottingham, *et al.*, IV, 40.
114 Ibid., 40.
115 Cf. *Principles of Philosophy*. I § 41. See also, Descartes' letter to Elizabeth, 3 November 1645. *AT* I, 332. Cf. *K*, 184.
116 B. Spinoza to Schuller, The Hague, October 1674. Cf. *The Chief Works of Benedict de Spinoza* (London 1901).

has created the nature of something in such a way that one cannot withhold one's consent when faced with the reality of this thing. We see this aspect of the foundation of the Cartesian science even better in the sixth meditation where divine truthfulness will be called on to guarantee not a clear and distinct idea, but a natural propensity. This natural propensity is what urges belief in the existence of external bodies, though in and of itself obscure and confused as are all instincts. However, unlike all other inclinations it is not correctable, just as assent to clear and distinct is irreversible.

4.4. *The Ends of God*

Once the genesis of error and human responsibility are clarified, it yet seems that the divine innocence has not been fully proved. After all, God could prevent the error one produces. "It was easy for God to make me in such a way that I never deceive myself ever, though remaining free and having limits to my knowledge." Yet again, one asks, why does God allow the occurrence of evil?

It is worth noting that before answering this question according to the templates of Augustinian-Thomistic theodicy, Descartes lays out an argument on the basis of which the question itself would no longer make sense. Descartes appeals to the unknowable quality of the "ends" of God, or God's purposes. If they are unknowable it is useless to wonder why God permitted error, or whether error is compatible with the divine project to create a better world. "There is considerable rashness in thinking myself capable of investigating the impenetrable purposes of God."[117]

This inclusion, even in its brevity, is hugely important, for on account of this Descartes can introduce a fleeting but incredibly demanding statement of the uselessness of teleology in physics. "For since I now know that my own nature is very weak and lim-

---

117 *Meditations* in *The Philosophical Writings of Descartes, Volume II*, John Cottingham, *et al.*, IV, 39.

ited, whereas the nature of God is immense, incomprehensible and infinite, I also know without more ado that he is capable of countless things whose causes are beyond my knowledge. And for this reason alone I consider the customary search for final causes to be totally useless in physics."[118] The illegitimacy of employing teleology to explain the phenomenon of the world is a principle enormously emphasized in Cartesian science. Yet again, a theory crucial to physics finds its justification in metaphysics.

The whole of Aristotelian physics is dominated by teleology, for only through the end does Aristotle think it is possible to explain the phenomenon of observable order in the world. That is, why cats give birth only to other cats, or why the seasons always unfold one after the other in the same order, or why almond plants always blossom in the spring. According to Aristotle, what chronologically falls at the end, or as the final development of some ordered phenomenon, explains this same development. The adult individual is what grows up from being a child, and so thereby defines the child. There is consistency in the reproduction among animals because the nature of a particular animal species guides and organizes the generation of each individual in that species. So in Aristotle, the alternative to the teleological explanation is chance, that all of this is random. But chance cannot explain order, therefore wherever there is order there is also teleology. Instead, for Descartes there is no need to invoke teleology in explaining the order existing in nature. The regularity in the phenomenon is completely explained with the crashing of particles of matter, moved according to the laws that regulate motion, or according to its efficient cause. This latter possibility surrounding the efficient cause was analytically played out in Descartes' fable of the formation of the world. Descartes counters "chance/disorder v. end/order" with mechanistic determinism, leaving teleology out of the order of the universe. In the fourth meditation, banishing teleology from physics is justified by the incomprehensibility of God. Descartes does not deny, as does

118 Ibid.

Spinoza, that God has an end, but he denies that man can know what it is. That is enough to declare teleology to be illegitimate in any scientific explanation.

In Cartesian science, the importance itself of the principle by which it is illegitimate to investigate the ends of God leads one to suspect that the authentic Cartesian position with respect to theodicy is exactly what Descartes fleetingly mentions here. That is, Descartes thinks the question of the compatibility of error and evil with the ends of God is out of place.

For the most part, the theory of the impracticality of this question is in harmony with the Cartesian theory of God's incomprehensibility, as well as the incommensurability of human and divine logic. What is the sense in asking a God who is beyond even the good and true and whose ends by definition cannot be grasped through human logic and values about the compatibility of error with the objective of creating the most perfect world possible? It is as if the ideal of perfection in the world was something to be accounted for by God, or realized, a perfection that placed itself before him, imposed itself on him. But no value can precede divine free will. What is good and perfect is such because God accomplishes it, and not vice versa. That is, one does not say that God does what he does because it is good and perfect. "God did not will the creation of the world in time because he saw that it would be better this way than if he had created it from eternity," says Descartes in his reply to the sixth objections. "On the contrary, it is because he willed to create the world in time that it better this way than if he had created it from eternity."[119]

The Jesuit Mesland presses Descartes on the meaning of having theorized that God in his choosing is guided by "what is better" in a system where God is beyond what for us is the good. Essentially, Descartes admits that here the question of the compatibility of error with the perfection of God's work makes no sense. "I do not claim to have ever proposed that God always

119 "Replies to the Sixth Set of Objections," in *The Philosophical Writings of Descartes, Volume II*, John Cottingham, *et al.*, 291.

does what he knows to be most perfect, and it seems to me that a finite mind cannot make judgments on this matter. But I have tried to clarify the difficulty in question, the cause of error, *supposing* that God has created the most perfect world. For supposing the opposite, this problem certainly raises it head."[120] This letter gives us a key to understanding the progression of theodicy in the fourth meditation. Immediately after having declared the ends of God to be unknowable, Descartes measures his position against the question of the compatibility of error with divine choice necessarily oriented towards what is best. Descartes decides not to explicitly put into play the theory of the free creation of eternal truths in the text of the *Meditations*. Instead he submits to the logic of traditional theodicy: If God intended to create the best possible world, why has he permitted something like error, which seems to eat away at the perfection of his work? The theodicy of the fourth meditation must therefore be interpreted as a kind of hypothetical theodicy. The meditator admits, though does not concede, that one can investigate the ends of God. Hence he supposes that God intended to create what is best, and so also that it makes sense to ask God for the reason behind the presence of error. And yet, even in this case it is possible to demonstrate God's innocence.

Therefore, God would have been able to ensure that men never fall into deception, regardless of the disproportion between the intellect and the will. He would have been able to grant clear knowledge even with the little that men know. Or he would have been able to make man firm in never judging if not of what is clearly and distinctly known. Why did God not utilize some means to avoid the generation of evil? The reply is reminiscent of something Augustine or Thomas might have said: the universe is more perfect if a part of it is flawed. "But I cannot therefore deny that there may in some way be more perfection in the universe as a whole because some of its parts are not

120 Descartes to Mesland, 2 May 1644. *AT,* IV, 113. Emphasis mine. Cf. *K,* 147.

immune from error, while others are immune, that there would be if all the parts were exactly alike."[121] God's initiative to create the best world is realized *because* of the presence of error in the world.

Error is therefore compatible with the truthfulness of God and no longer constitutes an objection with respect to the use of the divine guarantee of clear and distinct ideas. In obedience to the impulses of the mind, every time men are in a position of not being able to do anything but render consent, here they will have found the truth.

4.5. Some Observations of Method

We now have all the elements to better understand a characteristic of the *Meditations* mentioned earlier. As the arguments unfold, the intricate material of the first meditation is slowly unraveled. Let us go back for a moment to the theory of the omnipotent God invoked in the beginning of the meditations. "What is more, since I sometimes believe that others go astray in cases where they think they have the most perfect knowledge, (a) may I not similarly go wrong every time I add two and three or count the sides of a square, or in some even simpler matter, if that is imaginable? (b) But perhaps God would not have allowed me to be deceived in this way, since he is said to be supremely good. (c) But if it were inconsistent with his goodness to have created me such that I am deceived all the time, it would seem equally foreign to his goodness to allow me to be deceived even occasionally; yet this last assertion cannot be made."[122]

Here one hypothesizes that an almighty God made it so that I deceive myself even in the simplest operations as in (a). In (b), one responds to this in an attempt to thwart the deception by the fact of divine goodness. Lastly, in (c) one gives a rebuttal of (b) exhibit-

121 *Meditations* in *The Philosophical Writings of Descartes, Volume II,* John Cottingham, *et al.,* IV, 43.
122 *Meditations* in *The Philosophical Writings of Descartes, Volume II,* John Cottingham, *et al.,* I, 14.

ing the situations of error, thereby confirming the legitimacy of the doubt inspired by the theory of an almighty God. These short lines are a tangled mess of obscure and confused ideas, but they are sorted out in the third and fourth meditations. In the third meditation we see consistency given to the reply in (b)—deception is in conflict with divine truthfulness and therefore it is impossible. In the fourth meditation the position in (c) is dispelled, which otherwise serves to neutralize (b) and keep the theory of deception in (a) on its feet.

It is a good thing, then, to keep in mind that the process of meditating allows for the gradual clarification of its starting points, and so it can happen that only those advanced in the meditative process "clearly and distinctly" understand what the theories put in play at the beginning really imply. If it is only in the third and fourth meditations that the crux of the conflict between power, God's truthfulness (or goodness, according to the imprecise definition given in the first meditation), and the experience of error is sorted out, it is no wonder that it is not until the fifth meditation that one distinctly understands what the nature of the mathematics held in doubt really is. This is a crux that is insurmountable at the beginning of the meditations. The idea of God, in the name of whom mathematics is held in doubt, the nature of that which one doubts, and the modalities on account of which one can obtain distinct knowledge of mathematics are clarified along the unfolding of the work. So the reader has to wait until he has arrived at the clarifications of these points before clearly seeing the impossibility of continuing to feed a doubt that finds sustenance only in obscure and confused ideas. The place of maximum clarification of the whole complex of notions put into play at the beginning of the meditations in obscure and confused forms comes in the fifth meditation.

5. Inneism

The Essence of Material Things and the Existence of God

Descartes can now use the divine truthfulness demonstrated in the third and fourth meditations for his own purposes. The analysis of the piece of wax shows how what one knows clearly and distinctly of matter are only its geometrical-mathematical properties. But at the time of that analysis it would have been premature to derive conclusions of the essence of matter. There was not yet any guarantee that clear and distinct ideas were also true, and therefore that what one knows clearly and distinctly to be the essence of material things is true. But now, thanks to what we can say of divine truthfulness, it is possible to likewise say that what is known to be the essence of material things is, in fact, as we know it to be. That is, it is true.

5.1. *Inneism*

Mathematics is the example *par excellence* of clear and distinct knowledge, and it is made up exclusively of innate ideas. The theory that states that there are innate ideas in the mind is the basis for the entire theory of Cartesian knowledge. The claim of constructing a science independent from experience yet capable of adequately describing reality rests on this. Inneism is anticipated, albeit not in an organic fashion, in the third meditation where there is the analysis of the only idea, on that occasion, which is ascertained to have the character of an innate idea—the idea of God. Innate ideas, as opposed to adventitious ideas, do not involuntarily present themselves to the mind. And, as opposed to fictitious ideas, their content is for the mind inalterable and necessary. Descartes once again systematically takes up the inneist theory and unveils its ontological significance: unlike adventitious ideas, innate ideas describe reality independently from the being exemplified therein, and unlike made-up ideas they describe a reality which is independent from thought. Innate ideas denote immutable and eternal essences.

In order to establish whether an idea is innate or simply adventitious or made up, in the third and fifth meditations Descartes asks the reader to consider with him whether the mind is active or passive, first in conjuring up an idea, and then in the forming of the representative content of that idea. With respect to an idea presenting itself, the mind is active in situations of innate and made-up ideas (*I* decide whether to think of a triangle or formulate the image of a Pegasus), and passive in the event of adventitious ideas (it is not I who decides whether or not to see the sun when I open my eyes). Regarding the content of an idea, the mind is active in the case of made-up ideas (deciding whether or not to add wings to a horse) and passive in the case of innate and adventitious ideas (not deciding that the sum of interior angles in a triangle add up to one hundred and eighty degrees, nor that the sun is bright). One can better visualize this with the following schema on the basis of this crossing of characteristics:

	Innate Ideas	Adventitious Ideas	Made Up Ideas
An idea presenting itself to the mind,	the mind is... passive	active	active
Regarding the content of the mind,	the mind is... passive	active	passive

The theory of innate ideas relies on the resistance of a certain content of thought to the activity of the mind (as opposed to made-up ideas), though it still lacks some existing thing that imposes itself on the mind (as opposed to adventitious ideas). This is evident in Descartes' insistence of the fact that the content of an innate idea is not subject to arbitrary alteration. As he says, it is not possible to separate a triangle from its properties. This is merely a repetition from the point of view of the object of knowledge of what is already said in the fourth meditation from the point of view of the act of knowledge—judgment, always voluntary, can never be indifferent when faced with the truth. Descartes now finally explicates the theory of the non-manipulative nature of the content of innate ideas. The characteristics that belong to a being described by an innate idea are connected among themselves through logical implication. It is not possible to deny the being described by an innate idea one of these properties, for doing so causes the subject to fall into a contradiction. For example, it is not possible to avoid contradiction in denying that a triangle has internal angles equaling the sum of one hundred and eighty degrees. On the contrary, in made-up ideas I am free to take away or add properties that I put together in the moment that I forge this make-believe entity and bestow them upon this entity. In other words, I can think of a horse with or without wings.

Furthermore, Descartes now formulates additional criteria to distinguish innate ideas from those that are made-up. With innate ideas the logic of discovery is in full force. For example, in the case of a geometrical figure, geometry can follow up on the discovery of its qualities and continue to demonstrate theorems that were absolutely unknown when the definition of that figure was given for the first time, even though other geometers later discovered more properties of that same figure. Innate ideas are open-ended. Fabricated ideas, on the other hand, are closed off. One finds in them only what he himself sets in motion as he initiates the forging of some idea. The character of a literary work is made up only of the qualities bestowed on him by the author in the work itself. If Shakespeare never wrote about the color of Iago's eyes, we would never know anything about it.

Both categories of criteria show that an innate idea refers to something that *is,* independently of whether or not someone thinks it up or about it. It is at the disposal of he who, at some point in time, discovers it. The resiliency of the content of an innate idea with respect to the activity of the mind makes one hypothesize that the essences of things correspond to these ideas, independently of both their exemplification as well as the free acts of the mind. Herein the representative content of an innate idea is ontologically different from the representative content of obscure and confused ideas, both made-up and adventitious. Beyond as much as they are thought of, these ideas have no reality. In and of themselves, they are "pure nothing." Instead, the essences of things, even if they are not exemplified, are part of real being and are therefore differentiated from fictitious beings and obscure and confused ideas. After all, it is possible that essences of things exist. As Suarez says, "Sciences that consider things abstracting from their existence are not looking at entities of reason, rather at real entities. That is, they consider real essences not according to the condition held objectively in the intellect respective to these entities, but in and of themselves inasmuch as these entities or beings are capable of existing with those natures or properties."[123]

The essence of mathematics are principal examples of essences denoted by clear and distinct innate ideas. "I find within me countless ideas of things which even though they may not exist anywhere outside me still cannot be called nothing; for although in a sense they can be thought of at will, they are not my invention but have their own true and immutable natures. When, for example, I imagine a triangle, even if perhaps no such figure exists, or has ever existed, anywhere outside my thought, there is still a determinate nature, or essence, or form of the triangle which is immutable and eternal, and not invented by me or dependent on my mind."[124] But the idea of God manifests the same characteristics. "I perceive many other attributes of God, none of which I can remove or alter."[125] The foundation of mathematics upon innate ideas sets the Cartesian theory against both a theory of the empirical origin of these sciences, as well as against a theory that holds mathematics to be the fruit of human craft and ingenuity.

The Cartesian theory of geometry and mathematics is written into a revival of Platonism, and Descartes is well aware of this and opens up by looking back on the Platonic theory of recollection. "It seems that I am not so much learning something new as remembering what I knew before."[126] In the Cartesian theory, as

---

123 F. Suarez, *Disputationes metaphysicae*. XXXI, II, X.
124 *Meditations* in *The Philosophical Writings of Descartes, Volume II,* John Cottingham, *et al.*, V, 45.
125 Ibid., 47.
126 Ibid., 44.

in the Platonic, mathematics is the realm of discovery of something that is real independently of the fact that someone knows it. This justifies the analogy of the famous recollection theory that Plato theorizes in the *Meno*. Descartes' theorems draw heavily from the "world" of mathematics, like the theorem demonstrated by the slave boy in the *Meno* who evokes the memory of an experience in the past.

According to Descartes, as we have seen in the analysis of wax in the second meditation, the entirety of our experience is interwoven with innate ideas and without them experience itself would not be possible.

Descartes did not invent the theory that states that some ideas represent things that belong to real being (what exists, or at least can exist), while others represent things that do not exist and cannot exist—such as fictitious beings, negations and privations—and for Descartes even confused and obscure ideas of the senses. But Descartes confronts and resolves the problem of distinguishing the ideas of beings that correspond to true essences, or beings which can exist, from fictitious beings in an original way. Suarez, for example, inserts beings whose definition does not imply contradiction into the realm of real being, and at the same time excludes make-believe entities from this realm. But Suarez does not address the problem of clarifying why fictional entities like winged horses, though not signaling an obvious contradiction in their definition, are not part of real being and thereby not capable of existing. Descartes, on the other hand, engages this difficulty in the fifth meditation, interested in distinguishing in the most precise way possible the "true" beings or entities in mathematics from fictional beings, as well as debunking the claim that mathematics is the fruit of human art. For an idea to represent something that belongs to real being, it is not enough that the definition of that being does not imply contradiction. Otherwise, one risks the inclusion of a Pegasus and centaurs in the category of real being. The definition must pass the two additional tests stated above: an idea is innate when it is impossible to deny one of the elements of its make-up without falling into contradiction, and when one can still discover further properties which were unknown at the initial perception. Pegasus and the centaurs do not pass these tests, but triangles and squares do.

It follows from the theory of mathematics that the Cartesian theory of truth defines itself as the correspondence between thought and the *thing* thought. This correspondence between thought and the thing known is what the truth is built up with,[127] and now that we know the nature of mathematics, we know what it means to say that his demonstrations are true or false. The operations of mathematics are true when they adequately describe the real beings that they make reference to, indeed the essences of mathematics and geometry. If God is truthful, the mathematical essences cannot be unlike how my intellect gathers them to be. In the case of clear and distinct ideas, that something is true already implies a correspondence between thought and the thing thought, even if the very thing known is not exemplified in nature.

We are deep in the heart of the Cartesian project, and divine truthfulness and inneism disclose their true role—to guarantee that human science describes the real structure of the world, and at the same time that science can do so even with a complete lack of information of the real existence of the world. "And now," Descartes concludes, "(...) it is possible for me to achieve full and certain knowledge of countless matters (...) concerning things which belong to corporeal nature in so far as it can serve as the object of geometrical demonstrations which have no concern with whether that object exists (innumera ... de omni illa natura corporea, *quae est purae Matheseos objectum,* mihi plane nota et certa esse possunt)]."[128] One will better understand that this is

---

127 Cf. Descartes to Mersenne, 16 October 1639. *AT* II, 597. "This word 'truth' in its proper sense denotes a conformity between the object and the thought of this object." Cf. *K, 165.*
128 *Meditations* in *The Philosophical Writings of Descartes, Volume II,* John Cottingham, *et al.,* V, 49.

Descartes' main objective from the particular formulation that is now given to the principle of divine truthfulness. Divine truthfulness guarantees that "everything that I know clearly and distinctly belongs to a thing, actually does belong to it." Again, to a *thing*. Innate ideas, clear and distinct ideas, refer to *things*. They speak of reality, and their correspondence to reality is legitimized by divine truthfulness. Of course, if mathematics were a collection of made-up ideas, in this regard it would make no sense to invoke the divine guarantee. Ontologically speaking they would be nothing, they would have no reality outside of thought. If this were true, as Hobbes goes on to demonstrate, mathematics would not claim to speak of anything but how the mind knows the world and not how the world is truly constructed. The same threat of the omnipotent God in the first meditation is no threat to them. Even if a "true" mathematics existed whose model was used by God to create the world, the important thing is that mathematics generated by the human mind, which has never claimed to speak of how the world really is, might "function" in its description of the world. The theory of the deception on behalf of an omnipotent God and the role of divine truthfulness take on full meaning instead in light of the theory of inneism. If innate ideas denote essences that do not depend on the mind, and if God in his omnipotence had ensured that there was no correspondence between ideas and the essences of things, human knowledge would have claimed to speak of the world in vain. On the other hand, only God, in his truthfulness, can guarantee that innate ideas provide an adequate account of those essences. Replying to Arnauld, Descartes condenses the doubt in this way: "But one of the exaggerated doubts which I put forward in the First Meditation went so far as to make it impossible for me to be certain of this very point (namely *whether things do in reality correspond to our perception of them*)."[129]

129 "Replies to the Fourth Set of Objections," in *The Philosophical Writings of Descartes, Volume II*. John Cottingham, *et al.*, 159. Emphasis mine.

This, then, is the point: divine deception is truly something only a philosopher who claims that the ideas speak truth of how the world is made should fear. Now that one knows the nature of mathematics, the meditator is in the position to fully evaluate what risk science would run if God, other than being omnipotent, was not also truthful.

5.2. *The Essence of Material Things*

Until now, Descartes speaks of mathematics in and of itself, taking for granted that they describe the essence of matter. Perhaps Descartes thinks he has already demonstrated in the second meditation that what the human intellect knows as the constitution of the nature of matter are the essences described by mathematics, and that once it reaches divine truthfulness there are no obstacles to the realization that the essence of bodies is reduced to its quantifiable characteristics. Nevertheless, an argument in favor of the theory that states that mathematics describes the essence of matter is provided in the fifth meditation as well, even though quite hastily. Essentially, the argument is nothing more than a rapid sketch. "Quantity, for example, or 'continuous' quantity as the philosophers commonly call it, is something I distinctly imagine (...) I also enumerate various parts of the thing...."[130] For Descartes, the imagination is the faculty that by definition is delegated only for the knowledge of what is material. "For imagining," he writes in the second meditation, "is simply contemplating the shape or image of a corporeal thing."[131] The imagination always functions with images, or pictures, yet in a two-fold manner. On the one hand, it can call back and elaborate on images received through the senses. In this case the content is dependent on the senses. On the other hand, it can translate purely intellectual ideas into physical images like those in geometry. In this way it adjusts itself entirely to the characteristics of innate

130 "Replies to the First Set of Objections," in *The Philosophical Writings of Descartes, Volume II.* John Cottingham, *et al.*, 63.
131 Ibid., II, 19.

ideas, and that means it is able to decide *whether* to imagine them (for example, whether to imagine the figure of a triangle) but not *what* to imagine (the imagination does not decide whether the triangle has three sides). This explains why Descartes can expand clearness and distinction to the imagination, which otherwise seems to be reserved to ideas originating wholly in the intellect. "I distinctly imagine the quantity that philosophers commonly call continuous quantity." Precisely because of the capacity to translate the clear and distinct ideas of the intellect into mental images, here "distinction" is also attributed to the imagination. Through these characteristics, already largely analyzed in the *Regulae*,[132] the imagination plays a critical role, and can be taken up as the main character in a true and proper experiment that is quite crucial—what cannot be imagined, like the soul of God, surely is not material, while what can be imagined has to do with bodies. The figures of geometry can be translated into mental images and that is enough proof of their being the essences of bodies.

The intellect shows us that mathematics describes real essences, and the imagination that these essences adequately describe the nature of matter. But the intellect and the imagination united together can only ensure that matter can exist, but not that it actually does exist. The proof of the existence of matter can only be provided by the senses, as Descartes lays out in the sixth meditation.

5.3. The a priori *Proof of the Existence of God*

The fifth meditation contains a surprise. Parallel with the analysis of the essence of material things, it reopens the chapter on the demonstrations of the existence of God, setting up a new proof, an *a priori* proof that Kant later labels ontological. This proof is extremely simple. It utilizes the definition of God (God is the most perfect being) as its major premise, and has for its minor

132 *Rules for the Direction of the Mind*. Cf. the twelfth and fourteenth rule, in *The Philosophical Writings of Descartes, Volume I*, John Cottingham, *et al.*

premise the definition of existence (existence is a perfection). From this Descartes deduces that God exists, insofar as in the very denial of the existence of God contradicts the definition of God and thereby leads one into contradiction. "Hence it is just as much of a contradiction to think of God (that is, a supremely perfect being) lacking existence (that is, lacking a perfection), as it is to think of a mountain without a valley."[133] The special quality of this proof, even with respect to the other Cartesian proofs that also are centered on the idea of God, is in the demonstration of the existence of God beginning with only the definition of God. He who accepts this definition of God would then contradict himself if he later denied the existence of God.

Faced with a new proof of the existence of God, two questions arise. Why does Descartes think it necessary to provide a new demonstration of the existence of God, and why has this new demonstration been placed in this spot? A possible explanation for the second question is offered by the very same paradoxical combination of the essence of material things and the demonstration of the existence of God. One sees this in the title, "The Essence of Material Things, and the Existence of God Considered a Second Time." It is certainly paradoxical, since the ontological difference between God and matter is for Descartes obviously absolute. And yet this pairing is strongly motivated. The first reason that justifies it can be found in the structure of the new proof, which is built in close analogy to the structure of mathematical theorems, as well as science which as we have just seen deals with the essences of material things.

For Aristotle, mathematics was an example of a science wherein perfect scientific knowledge is possible. That is, it is knowledge that in its demonstrations takes up the cause of the *demonstrandum* as its premise. In the case of mathematics, the cause with which Aristotle concerns himself is the formal cause, the definition of the being from which cascade all of its properties, or effects.

133 *Meditations* in *The Philosophical Writings of Descartes, Volume II*, John Cottingham, *et al.*, V, 46.

Inasmuch as this kind of demonstration assumes for its premise the definition of the *demonstrandum,* it generates perfect science, or knowledge that reaches the essence of the thing demonstrated. The role that is supported by the definition of the figure in geometrical theorems is carried out by the definition of God in the demonstration of the existence of God: God is the most perfect being, and the existence of God is deduced from this definition, as the properties of a triangle are deduced from the definition of the triangle. The syllogism, which assumes the cause as the premise, is called *a priori* in Latin in that it assumes for its premise what comes prior, or first in the ordering. So, the demonstration of the existence of God, like the proofs in mathematics, is an *a priori* demonstration as opposed to the proofs present in the third meditation that look for the cause of the idea of God and thereby witness the idea of God to be an effect. For, in reality, the effect comes after its cause, is posterior to it, rendering these earlier proofs of an *a posteriori* character.

There is another reason why this new proof of the existence of God is placed here. According to Descartes, as in geometrical theorems, the validity of the proof depends on the fact that the idea of God, like the ideas of geometrical figures, is an innate idea and therefore corresponds to an essence that is independent from thought. One can better understand this if, together with some of Descartes' dissenters, one compares this Cartesian proof to the demonstration of the existence of God which in the theological tradition resembles it the most. In fact, the Cartesian proof in the fifth meditation calls to mind Saint Anselm's proof delineated in the *Proslogion,* literally invoked by Caterus who also reminds Descartes that it has already been definitively refuted by Saint Thomas. Caterus argues that Descartes resurrecting this argument can be likened to the resuscitation of a dead man. Anselm also assumes as the major premise for his proof the definition of God that holds that no one can think of greater being than God. He then argues that he who accepts such a definition could not deny the existence of such a being without contradicting this same definition. If the being whose greater cannot be thought of did not actually exist in reality, one could think of a second being that had all the same characteristics of that greatest being, with the additional quality of existence. This would render the second being greater. If so, one *can* think of a greater being than the being whose greater cannot be thought of, and this implies a contradiction. Aquinas, without naming Anselm, reproduces the proof and then rejects it, invoking the illegitimacy of inferring an existence outside of thought from an existence merely thought of (which is an obligatory attribute of God, once God is defined as a being whose greater cannot be thought of). Simply admitting that the definition of God leads one to think of God as existing does not imply that God actually exists outside the mind. Likewise, simply admitting that the Cartesian definition of God as the most perfect being leads one to think of God as existing does not mean that God exists in reality. "Given that everyone means to express with this name *God* (...) that which is such that nothing greater can be conceived of, it does not follow that with this one means to say that the thing signified by this name is a part of nature, but only that it falls within the apprehension of the intellect."[134]

Descartes answers Caterus in a seemingly surprising manner. He supports Aquinas against the argument that originates in Anselm, though at the same time maintains that his own argument, unlike that of Anselm, escapes the Thomistic critique.[135]

134 Thomas Aquinas. *ST,* I, 2, ad 1. Caterus also cites this in the "First Set of Objections", in *The Philosophical Writings of Descartes, Volume II,* John Cottingham, *et al.*, 68.

135 See "Replies to the First Set of Objections," in *The Philosophical Writings of Descartes, Volume II,* John Cottingham, *et al.*, 83. "The argument which he then puts forward as an objection to his own position can be stated as follows. 'Once we have understood the meaning of the word 'God,' we understand it to mean 'that than which nothing greater can be conceived.' But to exist in reality as well as in the intellect is greater than to exist in the intellect alone. Therefore, once we have understood the meaning of the word 'God' we understand that God exists in reality as well as in the understanding.' In this form the argument is manifestly invalid, for the only conclusion that should have been drawn is: 'Therefore, once

Essentially, the fifth meditation contains a preventive neutralization of this Thomistic critique, which Caterus brings back to the fore. "It does not seem to follow from the fact that I think of God as existing that he does exist. For my thought does not impose any necessity on things...."[136] This is the objection that Descartes subjected himself to in the fifth meditation, to which he replies, "But from the fact that I cannot think of God except as existing, it follows that existence is inseparable from God, and hence that he really exists. It is not that my thought makes it so, or imposes any necessity on any thing; on the contrary, it is the *necessity of the thing itself*, namely the existence of God, which determines my thinking in this respect."[137] In attributing existence to God, one is not claiming to pass from thought to things, and therefore to impose the laws of thought on a reality that can well enough ignore them. On the contrary, they are things that impose themselves on my thought in their necessity. It is the essence of the triangle that makes me think of the equivalence of its internal angles to two right angles, as it is the essence of God that makes me think of God as existing. The essences of things, like the inneist doctrine just demonstrated, are independent of thought. Their content is not modifiable according to whim, rather imposes itself on the mind. This is why the proof of the existence of God starting from the definition of God is unique and not duplicable for fictional beings that I have arbitrarily constructed as having existence—an

we have understood the meaning of the word 'God' we understand that what is conveyed is that God exists in reality as well as in the understanding.' Yet because a word conveys something, that thing is not therefore shown to be true. My argument however was as follows: 'That which we clearly and distinctly understand to belong to the true and immutable nature, or essence, or form of something, can truly be asserted of that thing. But once we have made a sufficiently careful investigation of what God is, we clearly and distinctly understand that existence belongs to his true and immutable nature. Hence we can now truly assert of God that he does exist.'"

136 *Meditations* in *The Philosophical Writings of Descartes, Volume II*, John Cottingham, *et al.*, V, 46.
137 Ibid. Emphasis mine.

existing lion, or the perfect body. If I attempted to deduce existence from a fictional being I would certainly fall into the error that Aquinas reprimands Anselm for committing—the error of holding on to the theory that thought can impose its own laws, or its own fancy, on reality. What is missing in Anselm's argument, and hence renders his conclusions vulnerable to Thomistic attacks, is the theory of inneism. This same theory is what the validity of Descartes' proof in the fifth meditation depends on. If the idea of God that serves as the premise to the proof is indeed an innate idea, it represents "a true and immutable nature." But as we know, true and immutable natures are part of real being, and so if one of these, including that of God, contains existence in itself, this existence is not *only* a thought of existence, but already an existence independent from the thought of it that imposes itself on thought. Hence the passage from the idea of God to the existence of God outside of the mind does not take an ontological leap from thought to being, or thought to thing, but acts according to how things truly are in reality.

For these reasons, the *a priori* proof cannot but be placed where it is, the place in the *Meditations* where the theory of the inneism is fully developed. Essentially, Descartes rushes to show how the idea of God passes the test of inneism that the essences of geometry have already ably overcome. The idea of God, similar to ideas in geometry, is made up of elements that cannot be separated from each other (I cannot separate its essence from its existence), and from this I can trace conclusions that are not explicitly present in the definition that I started with. And so here we are: existence is not explicitly named in the definition of God as the most perfect being.[138]

138 Nevertheless, Descartes must never have been completely satisfied with the way he argued the analogy between the idea of God and the idea of geometrical figures in the text of the fifth meditation, for in his reply to Caterus he admits that the difficulty in proving that the idea of God corresponds to a real nature is "considerable." In an attempt to better answer the test of inneism, Descartes no longer assumes as his definition of God as the most perfect being, but the

There are, then, two very good, systematic reasons for which the *a priori* proof must be placed in the fifth meditation and likened to an analysis of the essence of material things. Yet the question remains as to the motive behind Descartes demonstrating anew the existence of God. The fact is, despite the analogy to mathematics, the proof of the existence of God enjoys an epistemological privilege: the certainty of mathematics is not of the same caliber as the certainty of the existence of God, for the former depends on the latter. The privilege of the proof of the existence of God over the demonstrations of mathematics can be better and more easily appreciated once a proof of God's existence that reads like a mathematical theorem is produced. The analogy between mathematical theorems and the *a priori* demonstration of the existence of God, which is only possible here in this part of the text, allows for the construction of a new argument for the necessity of the metaphysical foundation of physics.

5.4. *The Existence of God and the Truth of Ideas*

The *a priori* proof for the existence of God is a kind of junction in the *Meditations*. For the reader who follows the meditative

most potent being. It is advantageous in that now the existence inferred from infinite potency is not included, nor even implied, in the definition of God. Cf. "Reply to the First Set of Objections," in *The Philosophical Writings of Descartes, Volume II*, John Cottingham, *et al.*, 83–85. Just the fact that existence might be included, even though implicitly, among the infinite perfections attributed to God in the definition the most perfect being, risks not allowing for an adequate distinction between the deduction of existence from the definition of God and the deduction, for example, of wings from Pegasus, or of not distinguishing the idea of God from some other made-up idea. The difficulty of such a proof is revealed, among others, by Gassendi. Cf. "Reply to the Fifth Set of Objections," in *The Philosophical Writings of Descartes, Volume II*, John Cottingham, *et al.*, 225. "When you listed the perfections of God you should not have included existence among them so as to reach the conclusion that God exists, unless you wanted to beg the question."

agenda, this proof is likened to the demonstrations of mathematics and authenticated with them: "But if the mere fact that I can produce from my thought the idea of something entails that everything which I clearly and distinctly perceive to belong to that thing really does belong to it, is not this a possible basis for another argument to prove the existence of God?"[139] Since the *a priori* demonstration of the existence of God has the same structure as the demonstrations of mathematics, he who maintains that these are true will have to judge as such this, too.

Nonetheless, because of the strong analogy between the *a priori* proof and mathematics, Descartes can introduce a new meditative route that is explicitly addressed to the reader who has not been following the previous stages. Let's take a mathematician who shares Descartes' theory of mathematics and who is comfortable with the certainty of his own demonstrations. In other words, let's take a scientist who maintains that the evidence of his own demonstrations is enough to guarantee the truth of science, and hence maintains that science is founded on its own merit and hence independent from metaphysics. Of him one asks only that he concede that the *a priori* proof of the existence of God have the same cogency as the demonstrations of mathematics, after which the proof is modeled. "Hence, even if it turned out that not everything on which I have meditated in these past days is true, I ought still to regard the existence of God as having at least the same level of certainty as I have hitherto attributed to the truths of mathematics."[140] Constructing the *a priori* proof in close analogy with mathematical demonstrations, Descartes obtains a very important initial result—any mathematician who shares Descartes' theory of mathematics cannot be an atheist. But this is only a preliminary result, and if he had stopped here the fifth meditation would have been reduced to an apologetic discourse. Instead, Descartes is interested in advancing, by way of the analogy between

---

139 *Meditations* in *The Philosophical Writings of Descartes, Volume II,* John Cottingham, *et al.,* V, 45.
140 Ibid.

mathematical theorems of the demonstration of the existence of God, something quite complex. He attempts to show the mathematician that if he cannot accept the existence of God his mathematics can never aspire to the rank of science and the perfect certainty that he attributes to it. Indeed, for Descartes the alternative based on the self-guarantee of science is unsustainable.

The existence of God is not only as equally certain as the mathematical demonstrations, but again, it is *more* certain since the certainty of mathematics depends on the truth of God's existence. It is certainly true that it is not possible to doubt these mathematical theorems in the instant when one holds them in attention, or in the instant one attempts their demonstration. Nevertheless, it is possible to doubt them when one only has the memory of having demonstrated a theorem and possesses only its conclusion, when one does not have the whole chain of the demonstration leading to that conclusion in front of him. It happens, then, that one creates a psychological space for the doubt of clear and distinct ideas, and it becomes possible to hypothesize that an almighty God exists who has created the human mind such that it is deceived even in what it knows clearly and distinctly. That is, that the origin of the human mind is so imperfect that there is no hope of ever being able to actually arrive at what is true. Only after having demonstrated that God exists and that he is not a deceiver is this doubt rendered impossible, for someone who had objected that Pythagoras' theorem could be false because an almighty God could have made it so that I am deceived would now answer that this hypothesis has been demonstrated false and now is unthinkable.

As without thinking directly of the truth of the most simple propositions but concentrating on divine omnipotence and the power to make it so that the human mind is deceived even in the clear distinct ideas one can doubt the truth of these propositions, likewise one can doubt the conclusions of theorems once one's attention loses sight of the chain of demonstration that lead to that conclusion. In both cases it is possible to create a psychological space for doubt, which can be filled up with a rational reason to doubt. The possibility of this marks the difference between psychological certainty and the truth. An atheistic mathematician can be certain enough of what he is demonstrating, in the moment in which he demonstrates it, but as soon as he moves on to the next demonstration he creates a psychological space in which it is possible to think of another reason to doubt the prior demonstration. Hence, the mathematician's knowledge will never be true science, only a collection of "vague and inconsistent opinions" whose indubitable character fluctuates and is limited in time.[141] Only when the mathematician is convinced that God exists and is not a deceiver—and it will have to convince him of it, being the identical structure of theorems and the *a priori* proof of the existence of God—will he have no reason to doubt what he knew, what he knows, and what he will come to know clearly and distinctly to be true. And inasmuch as the psychological space is created, this space cannot be filled up with good reasons to doubt, and so doubt will remain impossible, even psychologically.

5.5. *The Cartesian Circle*

In the distinction between actual evidence (indubitable) and the memory of evidence (dubious until it is proven that God exists), Descartes gives us, more than anywhere else in his reply to the second objections, the key to silencing the accusation, formulated here and later brought up again by Arnauld in the fourth objections, of having fallen into a vicious circle in his attempt to guarantee the truth of science with divine truthfulness. This accusation deals with one of the classic objections made to the Cartesian foundation of science. The accusation circularity in demonstrating the existence of God and with this guaranteeing the

141 Descartes to Regius, 24 May 1640. *AT* III, 65. "*Persuasion* is when there yet remains some reason that might move one to doubt. But *science* is when there is a persuasion that is derived from a reason so strong that one could never be moved by something stronger. Those who deny that God exists do not by any means have this." Cf. *K*, 74.

truth of clear and distinct ideas looks like this: God is called on to guarantee clear and distinct ideas. But the demonstration of the existence of God is accomplished through clear and distinct ideas. Well, it has to be one or the other. Either the clear and distinct ideas needed for the demonstration of the existence of God do not need to be guaranteed, but then no clear and distinct idea needs guarantee, so the demonstration is worthless. Or else clear and distinct ideas all need to be guaranteed but there is no way to guarantee them for nothing can guarantee that the clear and distinct ideas used in the demonstration of the existence of God are even true. Once laid on the table, the theory of a God who has created human reason to be incapable of truth is a theory too intense to be overcome using this very same human reason.

In response to this objection, Descartes makes it clear that perfect certainty coincides with the impossibility—psychological—of doubting something under any kind of condition, for the impossibility of doubting a proposition under any kind of condition is only a reality when it is impossible to conceive of any reason whatsoever of doubt: absolute psychological indubitability and normative indubitability coincide. Now, the impossibility of doubting under any condition whatsoever condition is reached in a different way in the case of axioms, which are confirmed instead of weakened by any attempt to place it in doubt, and in the case of the demonstrations that are drawn from them, through which one can think of a reason to doubt, until it can be demonstrated that God exists and is not a deceiver:

> First of all, as soon as we think that we correctly perceive something, we are spontaneously convinced that it is true. Now if this conviction is so firm that it is impossible for us ever to have any reason for doubting what we are convinced of, then there are no further questions for us to ask: we have everything that we could reasonably want. What is it to us that someone may make out that the perception whose truths we are so firmly convinced of may appear false to God or an angel, so that

it is, absolutely speaking, false? Why should this alleged 'absolute falsity' bother us, since we neither believe in it nor have even the smallest suspicion of it? (...) But it may be doubted whether any such certainty, or firm and immutable conviction, is in fact to be had. (...) Now some of these perceptions are so transparently clear and at the same time so simple that we cannot ever think of them without believing them to be true. The fact that I exist so long as I am thinking, or that what is done cannot be undone, are examples of truths in respect of which we manifestly possess this kind of certainty. For we cannot doubt them unless we think of them; but we cannot think of them without at the same time believing they are true, as was supposes. Hence we cannot doubt them without at the same time believing they are true; that is, we can never doubt them. (...) There are other truths which are perceived very clearly by our intellect so long as we attend to the arguments on which our knowledge of them depends; and we are therefore incapable of doubting them during this time. But we may forget the arguments in question and later remember simply the conclusions which were deduced from them. The question will now arise as to whether we possess the same firm and immutable conviction concerning these conclusions, when we simply recollect that they were previously deduced from quite evident principles (our ability to call them 'conclusions' presupposes such a recollection). My reply is that the required certainty is indeed possessed by those whose knowledge of God enables them to understand that the intellectual faculty which he gave them cannot but tend towards the truth.[142]

---

142 "Replies to the Second Set of Objections," in *The Philosophical Writings of Descartes, Volume II*, John Cottingham, *et al.*, 104–105.

The absolute indubitability of axioms that Descartes formulates here, though already utilized and operational in the first proof of the existence of God, is guided in its development by a presupposition that we know—that the axioms (except the particular and privileged axiom that is the *cogito*) say nothing of things. One generates a science only when one carries out demonstrations beginning with these axioms. Here one succeeds in talking about the reality beyond the mind, and thereby enters into the sphere of correspondence between thought and the things of which the truth consists. At this level one can usher in the doubt that demonstrations do not accurately describe reality, that they might be false. In the range of what is dubious, even as much as they are applications of the axioms, the very simple propositions such as 2+3=5 come back into play, of which we know can entertain doubt in an indirect manner, bringing them up under the category of "clear and distinct ideas."

In the case of these simple propositions, as well as in the case of the demonstrations, Descartes tries to carve out a real psychological space wherein it is possible to host reasons for doubt. In a direct way in the case of demonstrations, and indirectly when dealing with simple propositions, doubt has always been possible inasmuch as there has always been allowed the situation wherein a thinkable reason to doubt can be sustained. Again, there must always be a present and thinkable reason for doubt, however small. Herein lies the difference between a purely psychological certainty and the truth, according to Descartes. It is one thing to set up particular situations wherein doubt is psychologically impossible, for example to think of individual simple propositions or to have some particular demonstration before one's eyes. It is another thing altogether to be unable to invoke a rational reason to doubt something. The latter is that situation wherein a stable science is guaranteed, one that corresponds to the truth. In this sense, even the present evidence is held in doubt even if only indirectly, and as long as these doubts are possible the present evidence is not certain. But if one is able to convince himself that what appears to his mind to be true cannot appear false to any other mind, then what is indubitable must coincide with the truth. This indubitable character is what one arrives at with the demonstration of the existence of God and his truthfulness. Through this, the motive for doubt that once impeded the transformation of the evidence in a perfect science is now unthinkable. We no longer have any thinkable reason for doubt, nor any psychological space for the doubt one created, for this space is left empty and doubt will be psychologically impossible in any condition. Only now do the psychological impossibility of doubting and lack of reasons for doubting coincide.

But, one might say, the impossibility of conceiving that what is indubitable for me may also be indubitable for another mind is still and always a psychological impossibility, and who can guarantee me that truth corresponds with this impossibility? Who can guarantee that I do not deceive myself in the demonstrations of God and his truthfulness? Could my knowledge be totally false, including the conviction that valid reasons do not subsist to think that what appears as true to me to someone else's mind appears to be false? But I have come to the point in which this possibility, that is the possibility of the subjectivity of the whole of human knowledge, is inconceivable insofar as it is no longer backed by solid reasons and hence rendered senseless. The theory that science may be put into question by senseless questions is deemed in turn by Descartes to be senseless. He articulates this in his reply to the second objections, saying that what one is looking for is "a conviction so firm that it is impossible for us to have any *reason* for doubting what we are convinced of."[143] And once a belief of this kind is found, "there is nothing left to seek after, with regard to this we have all the certainty that we could reasonably want." After one demonstrates that God exists and that God is truthful and one does not succeed in finding any more reasons to doubt the evidence of it, we are no longer interested in the person who once

143 "Replies to the Second Set of Objections," in *The Philosophical Writings of Descartes, Volume II,* John Cottingham, *et al.*, 103. Emphasis mine.

imagined "that the perception whose truth we are so firmly convinced of may appear false to God or to an angel, so that it is, absolutely speaking, false. Why should this alleged 'absolute falsity' bother us, since we neither believe in it nor have even the smallest suspicion of it? For the supposition which we are making here is of a conviction so firm that it is quite incapable of being destroyed; and such a conviction is clearly the same as the most perfect certainty."[144] The theory of an absolute falsity in human science is interesting for as long as it is sustained by thinkable arguments. When it is no longer thinkable, there ceases to be a theory. It is not only the dogmatic that has to justify its own convictions. The skeptic, too, has an obligation: his doubt must be justified, under pain of otherwise becoming unacceptable.

Some interpretations maintain that in the above cited passage Descartes admits to being content with truth as coherence and does not aspire to an absolute truth. That is, he admits that there is such a thing as absolute truth but that in principle it is beyond our reach. On the contrary, Descartes, against the objectors that continue to present him with hypotheses that human knowledge is only an appearance, even if it is indubitable, is only claiming that if by truth as coherency one means the indestructible conviction that things are made as science describes them, then absolute truth is the same as this "coherency" and he challenges anyone who thinks he can demonstrate a deeper level of conceivable truth to do so. "Why should we exhaust ourselves for this absolute falsity, *for we do not believe in it.*" Descartes' vehement refusal to continue to doubt evidence even when there are no longer any thinkable reasons to do so highlights an important target in the foundation of science in the *Meditations*. They are, in fact, precisely the supposed "theologian" authors of the second objections that throw back the argument through which, in the first meditation, Descartes places clear and distinct ideas in doubt: "Cannot God treat man as a doctor treats the sick, or a father his children? In both cases—the objectors argue—there is frequent deception

144 Ibid.

though it is always employed beneficially and with wisdom. For if God were to show us the pure truth, what eye, what mental vision, could endure it?"[145] The deceiving God is not only a methodological artifice, but also incarnates a real threat that theology raises against science, when it claims that the truth is only accessible to the infinite mind—it is a threat that Descartes hopes now to have definitively dismantled. If demonstrations use only clear and distinct ideas and indubitable axioms, one will no longer have to fear that their conclusions appear true to our eyes only.

Is this answer convincing? On the whole, it seems not. For even in our own day we argue whether or not Descartes has fallen into a vicious circularity, and if his defense is a good one. One must try to understand the reason behind this persistent repositioning of the accusation, despite the multiplicity of the arguments with which Descartes' defense is attempted, even beyond those advanced by the author himself. Now then, the risk of the "vicious circle" in Descartes is intrinsic to the very project of founding the perfect science within the finitude of the human mind. In principle, this project excludes all contact with the divine mind. Not only are the truths of mathematics known inside the mind, but so is the idea of God and the knowledge of his existence. This aspect must have seemed so important to Descartes that in order to sustain it he did not hesitate to make a radical theological decision in favor of the theory that states the essence of God can be known through a created idea. As we know, Thomas Aquinas vehemently denies that the human mind can know the essence of God through a created idea. Aquinas and the whole of the Thomistic theological culture rejected the possibility of a perfect and demonstrative science of God, likened to what is theorized in the scientific Aristotelian syllogism. To find the premises of this Cartesian decision one must turn to the theology of Duns Scotus, who, against Thomas, asserts the possibility of representing the infinite through the finite. Descartes

145 "The Replies to the Second Set of Objections," in *The Philosophical Writings of Descartes, Volume II,* John Cottingham, *et al.,* 90.

falls decidedly on the side of Scotus: the human mind has clear and distinct knowledge of God, and can go so far as to demonstrate God's properties as one might demonstrate geometrical theorems, even without having direct contact with the divine essence. Yet the human mind knows God by way of a created idea. Knowledge itself of the infinite is hence listed by Descartes among the cognitive instruments which are proper to the finite mind, ideas, definitions, and *a priori* demonstrations. Clear and distinct ideas cannot be guaranteed if not through another clear and distinct idea. Finite science cannot utilize direct contact with the infinite and the absolute to guarantee itself. Hence, there will always be the risk of falling into this argumentative circle, as it is intrinsic to the Cartesian project. The accusation and Descartes' defense, then, will continue to follow each other throughout the commentary, even after the first exchange between Descartes and the second group of objections.

An alternative, however, seems to emerge from Descartes' decision to guarantee finite science with the knowledge of the infinite, as this knowledge can be obtained even within human finitude. Either one maintains that no one can claim anything beyond this or different than this guarantee while remaining within finite knowledge, thus rendering this to be an absolute truth. Or, one maintains that no one can claim anything further, nor anything different, so absolute truth must be out of the reach of the human mind. Of these two, Descartes decisively chooses the first. And it is this choice that deep down motivates the whole Cartesian imposition of the pursuit of the truth. What is true, as we know, coincides with the absence of valid grounds for doubting. The validity of these grounds, in turn, is weighed by human reason. If one had wanted to completely depart from the instruments with which reason evaluates any admissibility of doubt, and hence the validity of their dissolution, one would enter into a frame of mind in which the undertaking itself of the search for truth with the instruments reason is in possession of would be impossible—this is a frame of mind that Descartes consistently denies the "citizenship to philosophy."

The accusation of circular thinking has a good grasp of the fact that the guarantee of clear and distinct ideas is obtained through some other clear and distinct idea, and therefore that the guarantee of indubitable ideas occurs on the same level. But this is precisely the nature of the Cartesian project: to found science staying within the boundaries of the human mind. And this is the nature of the Cartesian response to the skepticism of theologians: doubts as to human knowledge are admissible as long as they are backed by arguments that human reasons judges to be well founded.

After Descartes, and contrary to Descartes, Malebranche and Spinoza return to look for the guarantee of the veracity of human knowledge in the direct contact with the divine, holding as manifestly inadequate the delicate balance in the Cartesian foundation of science by way of a finite and created idea (capable of representing infinity), in the ordering of separation between the human and divine mind.

6. The Mind and the Body

Once the nature of bodies is clearly and distinctly known, one also knows that bodies can exist since God is "capable of creating everything that I am capable of perceiving [clearly and distinctly]."[146] The sixth meditation is dedicated to demonstrating that bodies exist and, in particular, that the body which I call my own exists. Furthermore, despite its intimate union with the mind, it is truly distinct from spiritual substance.

6.1. *Real Distinction*

With respect to what we already know in the second meditation, two later acquisitions make a demonstration of the real distinction between the mind and the body possible only now: the divine truthfulness that guarantees that if the mind and the body

146 *Meditations* in *The Philosophical Writings of Descartes, Volume II*, John Cottingham, *et al.*, V, 50.

are clearly and distinctly conceived of as two separate substances, in effect they are, and the knowledge of the nature of the body. The latter, the knowledge of the nature of the body, offers a kind of verification of what we already know following the knowledge of the nature of the mind, obtained in the second meditation. Now that we know the nature of the body, we know not only that the mind is conceived of as a complete thing apart from the body, but also that the body is conceived of as a complete thing independent from the mind. As thought is the attribute that allows knowledge of the capacity of the self to subsist independently from all else, likewise extension is the attribute that allows knowledge of the capacity of the body to subsist independently from the mind. And since divine truthfulness guarantees the truth of clear and distinct ideas, I can finally confirm that it is not only by my knowledge, but also because of the ordering of things, that the mind and the body are two distinct substances.

Now, it is possible that God has decided to unite the mind and the body in such a way that they never subsist separately of one another. But since God has the power to generate all things that I distinctly conceive of, and since I can distinctly conceive of the mind as a substance even without the body, and the body as a substance even without the mind, I can be sure that despite their actual union the mind and the body can be separated "at least through the omnipotence of God." Therefore, the fact of their actual union does not hinder the fact that they still are two substances truly distinct from one another.

The theological argument that attests to the real distinction between the mind and the body is constructed in this way:

Divine omnipotence can do everything that I clearly and distinctly conceive of.

I clearly and distinctly conceive of the mind and the body as two distinct substances.

Therefore, the mind and the body can be separated at least through this divine power.

"The question of what kind of power is required to bring about such a separation does not affect the judgment that the two things are distinct," adds Descartes.[147] The Cartesian argument conducts itself according to calls for differing modalities of divine power. Here Descartes refers to the traditional distinction between an absolute power and ordered power of God.[148] Absolute power is what God can do considering his power in itself, independent of all other attributes. Ordered power is what God can do considering the whole of his power and his decrees or power combined with his will. The divine decrees limit the exercise of God's potency, in the sense that some things that God could have accomplished through his absolute power (that men would not die, for example) are impossible to carry out considering the choice to establish things differently. Naturally, divine choices do not strip God of his naturally attributed power. In absolute power, God can always make it so that men do not die, in the sense that the capacity to do so remains in God.

Descartes is reasoning from the inside of this problem. The mark of real distinction is being able to conceive of each of the two substances separately without contradiction. This way of conceiving of them corresponds with the capacity of God to separate them, since God can do anything that seems to the human mind to be possible (not contradictory). Yet it is possible that, in his ordered power, God has established the mind and the body as united in such a way that one can never exist without the other for the duration of human life, and hence it is impossible for God, in his ordered power, to make the body exist without the mind and vice versa for as long as a human being is alive. Nevertheless, this does not inhibit God from conserving the power to enact this separation. So, in absolute power, it is always true that "[the mind and the body] can always be set up separately, at least through the omnipotence of God."

147 Ibid.
148 *Translator's Note:* Here the reference is to the classical *potentia absoluta* and *potentia ordinata.*

6.2. *The Immortality of the Soul*

"I am not saying that one of these days I won't finish a small *Treatment of Metaphysics,* which I started in Frisia and whose principal objective is proving the existence of God and our souls when they are separated from the body, hence also proving their immortality."[149] These are Descartes' words to Mersenne in 1630. While he composes the *Meditations,* Descartes is still certain that he would demonstrate the immortality of the soul, as it is even written into the title of the first Latin edition: *Meditationes de prima philosophia, in qua Dei existentia et animae immortalitas demonstrantur.* But the reference to the immortality of the soul disappears in the subsequent edition, which more modestly limits itself to pronouncing the intention of demonstrating the distinction between the soul and the body: *Meditationes de Prima Philosophia, in quibus Dei existentia, et animae humanae a corpore distinctio demonstrantur.* And not only this, Descartes asks Mersenne to add to the title of the second meditation ("The Nature of the Human Mind") the words "and How It Is Better Known than the Body" in order to prevent the reader from thinking that in this meditation he proposes to demonstrate the immortality of the soul.[150]

In his Preface to the *Meditations,* Descartes clarifies that only one of the premises necessary in proving the immortality of the soul is set down in the second meditation, the "concept of the soul which is as clear as possible and is also quite distinct from every concept of body." But this is not enough. "A further requirement is that we should know that everything that we clearly and distinctly understand is true in a way which corresponds exactly to our understanding of it; but it was not possible to prove this

---

149 Descartes to Mersenne, 25 November 1630. *AT* I, 182. Cf. *K,* 19.
150 Descartes to Mersenne, 28 January 1641. *AT* III, 297. "To the title of the second meditation, *Of the Nature of the Human Mind,* one can add, *That It Is More Known than the Body,* so that one is not led to believe that herein I want to prove the immortality of the mind." Cf. *K,* 94.

before the Fourth Meditation. In addition we need to have a distinct concept of corporeal nature, and this is developed partly in the Second Meditation itself, and partly in the Fifth and Sixth Meditations. The inference to be drawn from these results is that all the things that we clearly and distinctly conceive of as different substances (as we do in the case of the mind and the body) are in fact substances which are really distinct one from the other; and this conclusion is drawn in the Sixth Meditation."[151] Nevertheless, not even these premises are enough to prove the immortality of the soul. Other theories that one does not find in the *Meditations* must be added to them in that "they depend on the explanation of the whole of physics." In the first place, one has to know that substances are by their very nature "incorruptible." Through interaction with other finite beings, the accidents of finite beings are modified, but the substance that these accidents belong to can be annihilated by the will of God alone. In Descartes, the material world is composed of a single substance, a substance indefinitely extended. The human body, like any body, is not a substance but only a particular configuration of matter. Therefore, the human body is an accident of extended substance. When that particular configuration of extended substance that is the human body is lost, the human body itself is annihilated. But the extended substance which the human body is a mode of is not annihilated. The human being dies, but the extended substance does not perish. Inasmuch as it is a substance, this cannot be annihilated if not by God himself. In death, there is no annihilation of any substance. The spiritual universe, however, is composed of a plethora of substances, as many substances as there are human beings. As death does not imply the annihilation of the bodily substance, all the more reason to say that it does not annihilate the thinking substance. "The human body is no longer itself, hence only the configuration of some of its parts is noticeably altered." This is why it "can easily perish," while the human soul "is always (...) the

151 "Synopsis of the Following Six Meditations," in *The Philosophical Writings of Descartes, Volume II,* John Cottingham, *et al.,* 9.

same soul," despite the changes that take place in the mind. As opposed to the body, the soul is "of its nature immortal."[152] Personal identity, which the self consists of, is assured of the mind inasmuch as it is a substance, and is in no way interested in the particular modifications of the corporeal substance that we categorize as death.

On the whole, the demonstration of the real distinction between the mind and the body contained in the *Meditations* that means to advance the immortality of the soul is too much, yet too little. Too much in that death brings no annihilation of the corporeal substance and so the death of the body affects no substance, neither corporeal nor spiritual. It is too little in that the real distinction is insufficient to demonstrate the immortality of the soul if one does not add the fact that substances are by their very nature immortal. Nonetheless, there is no doubt that real distinction demonstrates that everything that happens to the body does not in any way touch the soul, and this is enough "to give mortals the hope of an after-life."[153]

6.3. The Existence of Material Things

One cannot ask what a thing is if one does not know if it is. The question as to the existence of a thing precedes any investigation of the nature of that thing. Aristotelian empiricism conducts itself along these lines.[154] Descartes overturns this presupposition in all its aspects and wherever it is planted. The existence of one's self has been traced to the depth of one's nature. The existence of God is demonstrated starting from the knowledge of his essence, and by now we know everything about material things, except whether or not they exist.[155] The last pages of the *Meditations* are

152 Ibid., 9.
153 Ibid., 10.
154 Aristotle, *Posterior Analytics*, II, 8, 93a, 20–21. "It is impossible to know what a thing is, while passing over whether it is."
155 Gassendi does not subscribe to the analysis of the piece of wax. For him it demonstrates the existence but not the essence of one's self. Descartes replies that the very knowledge of the existence of one's

dedicated to this residual problem, considered by Descartes to be marginal in the foundation of science even though they are the constitutive premise of every scientific investigation in Aristotle.

Descartes demonstrates the existence of bodies by way of ideas acquired through the senses. A preliminary attempt, accomplished using the imagination, shows itself to be uncertain. The imagination participates in the content of the pure intellect, but knows this content in a different way. It is capable of translating the concepts of geometrical figures of an intellectual origin into mental images through the sheer force of concentration. "When I imagine a triangle, for example, I do not merely understand that it is a figure bounded by three lines, but at the same time I also see the three lines with my mind's eye as if they were present before me; and this is what I call imagining."[156] The different modality

self depends on the knowledge of the nature of one's self. In fact, the existence of one's self is demonstrated by way of its principal attribute—thought. "I am surprised that you should say here that all my considerations about the wax demonstrate that I distinctly know that I exist, but not that I know what I am or what my nature is; *for one thing cannot be demonstrated without the other.*" Cf. "Reply to the Fifth Set of Objections," in *The Philosophical Writings of Descartes, Volume II*. John Cottingham, *et al.*, 248. Emphasis mine. Stressing the necessity of knowing the nature of God in order to prove his existence, in his reply to Caterus, Descartes attempts to demolish the Aristotelian precepts: "According to the laws of true logic, we must never ask about the existence of anything until we first understand its essence." Cf. "Reply to the First Set of Objections," in *The Philosophical Writings of Descartes, Volume II*, John Cottingham, *et al.*, 78. The fifth meditation closes after drawing upon a knowledge of the properties of bodies independently of the knowledge of their existence: "And now it is possible for me to achieve full and certain knowledge of countless matters (...) and also concerning things which belong to corporeal nature in so far as it can serve as the object of geometrical demonstrations which have no concern with whether that object exists" (French edition). Cf. *The Philosophical Writings of Descartes, Volume II*, John Cottingham, *et al.*, V, 49.

156 Ibid., 50.

through which the imagination and the intellect know the same thing would be easily explainable if there existed a body which the mind could apply itself to when it imagines and translates these intellectual ideas into images. Nevertheless, this reasonable explanation of the differences that are interwoven into the imagination and the intellect render the existence of bodies quite probable but not certain. In this case, the content of the imagination and the pure intellect is the same, hence the object of the act of imagining closely depends on pure intellection, that is, on an act of the understanding that is on the whole independent from corporality. The simple diversity in the modes of knowledge of content most assuredly of immaterial origin is judged to be a crucial clue, but still not definitive enough to demonstrate with certainty that bodies exist.

But the imagination does not exhaust its functions with translating the ideas of the pure intellect into mental images. In fact, it uses the memory to translate these ideas while freely combining them with material gathered from the senses. In this case, the imagination utilizes content that comes from a faculty that does not have any synchronization with the pure intellect. The imagination is a kind of Janus Bifrons. On one hand the imagination just refers back to the pure intellect, and so it appears ill-equipped to convince one of the existence of bodies. On the other hand, the imagination just refers back to the senses, and these faculties are what interest us here and now. Inasmuch as sensations cannot be explained through the pure intellect, these will give us the definitive proof of the existence of bodies.

When Descartes attempts to break the boundaries of his own thought through adventitious ideas in the third meditation, he rejects as not convincing all the reasons that spontaneously lead him to say that something outside of thought corresponds to (and so causes) these thoughts. Later, once divine truthfulness is ascertained, Descartes reexamines this reason. The passiveness of the mind, in the perception of adventitious ideas, does not seem convincing insofar as the mind might possess a hidden faculty that one is not aware of that causes these ideas. But now that a truthful God guarantees that what I clearly and distinctly perceive to be the nature of my own self to be truly so, I cannot doubt that if I possess a faculty of this kind I would be aware of it in that nothing takes place in my thought that goes unnoticed by my own self. The passivity of the sense faculties therefore implies the presence of an active power that may cause the sensations, and if this potency does not belong to one's self inasmuch as one's self is a thinking substance, this potency cannot be but in God or in external bodies. In deciding between these two possibilities, Descartes wields a reason which in the third meditation does not seem sufficient to demonstrate the existence of external bodies—the strong tendency to believe in their existence, and furthermore this as the cause of adventitious ideas. This is taken up once again as a reason and this time it is enough to dispel the theories that state that the ideas from the senses are caused by God. If it were so, God would have given man a propensity both invincible and untrickable to believe in the existence of bodies, and the impossibility of correcting this propensity would render God guilty of deception. Divine truthfulness yet again provides the means to discriminate between doubts that are no longer real (such as, I could have a hidden faculty that causes my sensations, or that the propensity to believe in the existence of bodies could be wrong) and doubts that still retain some legitimacy.

Descartes declares even the doubt that is worked up in the dream theory to be overcome using this same principle. There are certain signs that mark one's waking from a dream—the coherency and constancy of the images of the waking moment with respect to the rhapsody of oneric images in a dream, for example. Again, God would be deceiving him if this obvious difference in his perceptions of things did not correspond to a difference in reality.

However, the persistence of the legitimacy of other doubts does not permit the recovery of all the certainty of the common sense (the popular sense) surrounding external bodies. It is by no means said that these bodies are similar to the sensations that represent them. Here, the tendency that bears one to believe that there might be a likeness between the ideas of bodies and the bodies themselves is merely a prejudice acquired over time and not a natural propensity. So much so that the mind, in fact, is bestowed with a faculty delegated to the true knowledge of bodies—the pure intellect that can combat obscure ideas of the senses and correct them using its clear and distinct ideas.

As one can see, once the divine guarantee has come forth out of a knowledge of essences, it is called on to single out sections of truth within an obscure and confused world of natural inclinations. For Descartes, there is no contradiction in this even if it seems to be so in some of his contemporaries and disciples, including Malebranche. God does not simply guarantee the truth of the clarity and distinction in and of itself, but also the fact that it is not possible to reject the truth of clear and distinct ideas. The divine guarantee is legitimately invoked each time the inclination to believe is as formidable and invincible as it is in the case of clear and distinct ideas. In other words, God would be a deceiver if, having given to man an undefeatable tendency to believe in the truth of something, that something turned out to be false. This is why Descartes declares himself to be convinced that "everything that nature teaches me," and so not only clear and distinct ideas, "contain some truth." On these grounds Descartes not only can establish that external bodies exist, but also that a body is in a certain way united with the mind, and this is what I call "my" body. The localization of pain and pleasure in a particular body is a sufficient reason to declare a body to be "mine."

6.4. Substantial Union

The fact that there exists a body that is united in a particular way to the mind poses the problem of what kind of union this might be between the two substances, two substances which have been determined by intellectual knowledge to be truly distinct. On this point, Descartes realizes that he has to consider two models. The first is the Aristotelian model, that the mind is the form of the body, and that together the mind and body form a single substance. The second is that of Plato, that the mind and the body are two distinct substances, the center of one's self being his soul that, as Arnauld says with trepidation, "makes use of the body."[157] Of course, Arnauld harbors no doubt that, given the Cartesian premises, the model selected by Descartes is the Platonic. Yet Descartes feels compelled to draw from both Aristotle and Plato. The Platonic model (the real distinction between the mind and the body) is essential in providing an anthropological foundation to inneism and overcoming empiricism. The real distinction between the mind and body makes a clear and distinct knowledge that does not originate in the senses possible, and provides an anthropological justification for inneism. Nevertheless, the Platonic model does not succeed in explaining how the mind, apart from possessing a bundle of clear and distinct innate ideas, hosts other confused and obscure ideas that come from the senses. If Plato is right, the mind would never fall into error while judging the outside world. The Platonic model proves to be too much. It makes the human mind out to be quasi-angelic and does not explain the inclination towards error.

To explain the presence of obscure and confused ideas of the senses in the mind, one has to take a walk through the Aristotelian model of the substantial union between the body and the soul.

> Nature also teaches me, by these sensations of pain, hunger, thirst and so on, that I am not merely present in my body as a sailor is present in a ship, but that I am very closely joined and, as it were, intermingled with it, so that I and the body form a unit. If this were not so, I, who am nothing but a thinking thing, would not feel pain when the body was hurt, but would perceive the damage purely by the intellect, just as a sailor perceives by sight if anything in his ship is broken. Similarly, when the body needed food or drink, I should have an explicit understanding of the fact, instead of having confused

157 "Replies to the Fourth Set of Objections," in *The Philosophical Writings of Descartes, Volume II,* John Cottingham, *et al.,* 160.

sensations of hunger and thirst. For these sensations of hunger, thirst, pain and so on are nothing but confused modes of thinking which arise from the union and, as it were, intermingling of the mind with the body.[158]

The route Descartes takes is therefore that of assuming both the Platonic model of the two distinct substances as well as the Aristotelian model of the substantial union. The mind and the body are substances truly distinct, and so intellectual ideas do not originate in the senses. But, then again, because the type of union between the mind and the body is not as Plato describes it, which Thomas Aquinas in his use of an analogy proposed by Aristotle translated into the metaphor of the captain at the helm,[159] Plato is still wrong. The kind of union that exists between the mind and the body instead resembles what is theorized in Aristotle—they are united in such a way as to form a true and proper third substance. Only in this way can the obscure and confused ideas of the senses be explained. Both Plato and Aristotle have gathered a part of the truth. Aristotle sees only the union, and thereby erects confused and obscure ideas as a model of the truth. Plato sees only the distinction, and does not know how to provide a convincing explanation of error. Instead, Descartes comes up with a theory that God has instituted such a close union between the mind and body that a true and proper third substance is formed. Hence, he ably explains how the geometrical messages that the body receives from the outside, modifying its own form according to interactions with other bodies, translate themselves into sensations wholly dissimilar to their cause. The total heterogeneity between the two substances so closely aligned still remaining, it follows that a message from one comes translated totally heterogeneous in the other. There is some paradoxical irony in what Descartes concedes

158 *Meditations* in *The Philosophical Writings of Descartes, Volume II,* John Cottingham, *et al.,* VI, 56.
159 Cf. Aristotle, *De anima,* 413a8–9; Thomas Aquinas, *Summa contra gentiles,* II, 57, §2.

to Aristotle. The kind of union between the mind and the body that Aristotle uses to justify the truth of empiricism is taken up by Descartes to explain the origin of error.

If the reasons urging Descartes forward in these forays into Plato and Aristotle are obvious, it is likewise evident how difficult it is to conceptualize these. So much so that Descartes comes to the point of admitting the contradiction in the thought, following up on the naïve and cheeky words of the princess Elizabeth whose place as the celebrated beginner in philosophy gave her the opportunity to declare herself too stupid to understand the interaction between two heterogeneous substances.[160] Descartes borders on admitting the contradiction for the mind with respect to the theory of substantial union and the theory of real distinction.[161] Nevertheless, if the latter is the result of clear and distinct knowledge, the other is an "instruction from nature," indubitable internal experience, and as such it, too, is guaranteed by God. One can see that the divine guarantee of the indubitable character also comes to the point of producing something that seems contradictory to the mind, guaranteeing two conflicting truths—one based on the indubitable character of internal experience (pre-philosophical), and the other on the indubitable character of the clear and distinct ideas of the intellect.[162] This aspect, explicitly

160 Elizabeth to Descartes, 10/20 June 1643. *AT* III, 683.
161 Cf. Descartes to Elizabeth, 28 June 1643. *AT* III, 693. "It does not seem to me that the human mind is capable of really conceiving distinctly of the distinction between the mind and the body, and likewise of their union. The reason being that it is necessary to conceive of them as a whole, a single thing, and yet as they are two things, but this is contradictory." Cf. *K*, 142.
162 Ibid., 693–94. "Supposing that Your Highness still had in mind the reasons that prove the distinction between the body and the soul, and not wanting that the mind should lose them, to represent to yourself the notion of the union that everyone feels in himself even without philosophizing, that is, that he is one, single person, that has a body together with thought, which are each of such a nature that that thought can move the body and perceive the events that the body is subject to...." Cf. *K*, 142.

aporetic of the Cartesian system, is indeed the anthropological foundation of the entire edifice of science.

Descartes is prepared to respond with his usual architectonic breadth to at least one objection. The substantial union between the mind and the body is necessary in explaining the obscure and confused ideas that come from the senses. Very well. But why has God joined the body and soul in this way, if there seems to be such a clear disadvantage in doing so, at least from a theoretical perspective? Does not this type of union conflict with divine truthfulness? It is true that the obscure and confused ideas of the senses can be corrected through the pure intellect, but, even for this reason God cannot be accused of deception, he certainly does not appear to have labored in the interest of truth. It rather seems that he is engaged in rendering the pursuit of truth as difficult as possible for man. Even if one cannot accuse God of deception, one can neither say that God moves in active favoritism for the victory of the truth.

The cognitive end of the mind-body union is strongly emphasized by Aristotelians as a point of real superiority of empiricism over Platonists. If Plato is right, Thomas Aquinas observes, and true knowledge originates through innate ideas, the union of the body and the soul would not only be useless, but in some cases actually counterproductive.[163] Aristotelian Empiricism is much better adapted to the psychophysical constitution of man than is Platonic inneism. The argument for the end (teleological) of the mind-body composite is therefore a heavy argument against the

---

163 Thomas Aquinas, *ST,* I, 84, ad 4. "But according to this position, one cannot establish a sufficient reason whereby our mind is united to the body (...) If the mind, according to its nature had been constituted in such a way as to receive intelligible species only from distinct beings and not from the senses, there would no need for the body to understand, *rendering the union between the body and soul useless.*" (Emphasis mine.) Cf. Article 3 of this same question: "But if we establish that the union with the body is natural to the mind, there is a new difficulty. That is, that the natural operation of some thing is utterly impeded by what is natural to it."

Platonic theory of knowledge. Descartes must have felt how urgent a response to the Aristotelian was on this point. The Cartesian theory, in fact, that for the most part denies the plausibility of sensible knowledge, risks being beat up on a playing field that it set up for itself—that of divine truthfulness. The truth of sensible knowledge, asserted by Aristotelians against the Platonists, seems more in line with the truthfulness of God, which, in this case, would have planned the mind-body union in such a way as to ensure the possibility of true knowledge.

Perhaps it is the urgency to provide an alternative explanation equal to the force of Aristotle's that pushes Descartes to accept the challenge of explaining the end of the mind-body union. We must remember that the theory claiming that God made the best possible world is a premise assumed by Descartes in the fourth meditation as he tries to explain the phenomenon of error using this same premise. It is not, then, the first time that Descartes moves along the inside of this perspective, he who also declares aloud the illegitimacy of an inquiry of the ends of God. Yet, the difference is that Descartes, in the fourth meditation, assumes a teleology "in progress" and, so to speak, hypothetical. He supposes, yet does not concede, that God has advanced what is best, showing that notwithstanding this hypothetical premise that renders things more difficult, it is possible to justify God when confronted with the presence of evil in the world. Now, the question as to the end of the mind-body union lacks all tact and care, and teleology is actually taken up as a legitimate perspective within the extremely particular space of the reality constructed by the mind-body union. Only where nature entails consciousness, that is in the confined and particular space of the substantial union of the body and soul, is it acceptable to inquire after the ends of God: "For the proper purpose of the sensory perceptions given me by nature is simply to inform the mind of what is beneficial or harmful for the composite of which the mind is a part...."[164]

164 *Meditations* in *The Philosophical Writings of Descartes, Volume II,* John Cottingham, *et al.,* VI, 57.

The premises in responding to the question of the reasons why God united the mind and the body together in this way and why he did not instead employ some means similar to the Platonic model (much more favorable to clear and distinct knowledge) are actually set forth by Descartes beforehand when he elaborates on the proof of the substantial union of the mind and body. It is the emotions and feelings induced in the mind by particular modification in the body that proves that the mind has no extrinsic relation to the body. "Nature teaches me by these sensations of pain, hunger, thirst and so on, that I am not merely present in my body as a sailor is present in a ship, but that I am very closely joined and, as it were, intermingled with it, so that I and the body form a unit."[165] Proof of the substantial union is given by the transformations of the body's modifications into pleasing or painful feelings, which in turn ensure that one locates pain in the part of the body where this modification is determined. Feelings, then, prior even to the perceptions of the qualities of objects, prove what kind of union there is between the mind and the body. "For these sensations of hunger, thirst, pain and so on are nothing but confused modes of thinking which arise form the union and, as it were, intermingling of the mind with the body."[166] The transformation of some of the modifications of my body into these particular feelings is instituted by nature "to simply inform the mind of what is beneficial or harmful for the composite of which the mind is a part."[167] If God, in putting together the mind-body composite, adopted the Platonic model, we would prove neither hunger, nor thirst, nor pain. We would not be inclined to think that there is something like pain in a certain part of the body, and this would make us wiser though less solicitous in taking care of the health of the composite itself. The end that the divine operation seeks to realize in joining together the mind and the body in a certain way

165 *Meditations* in *The Philosophical Writings of Descartes, Volume II.* John Cottingham, *et al.*, VI, 56.
166 Ibid.
167 Ibid., 57.

is, then, wholly practical. Hence, one might say that God has been, yet again, truthful in the sense that the feelings roused up in the mind by the modifications of the body truly indicate what is helpful and what is harmful to the composite. These feelings *speak the truth* even if wholly confined to the realm of practicality. "There is nothing that my own nature teaches me more vividly than that I have a body, and that when I feel pain there is something wrong with the body, and that when I am hungry or thirsty the body needs food and drink, and so on. So I should not doubt that there is some truth in this."[168]

Certainly, this union enacted for the better conservation of the mind-body composite later on elicits a negative relapse in the speculative sphere in that it becomes evident that everything that passes through the body is transliterated into another language in the mind. For example, movement is translated into sound or color. However, on this plane man is not guided by an invincible natural instinct. Man is instead endowed with a faculty, the pure intellect, capable of opposing the inclination to objectify the sensations to think that colors are really in objects. This is not a natural inclination, however, rather acquired during childhood and hence it is always possible to suppress it. "My nature, then, in this limited sense, does indeed teach me to avoid what induces a feeling of pain and to seek out what induces feelings of pleasure, and so on. But it does not appear to teach us to draw any conclusions from these sensory perceptions about things located outside us without waiting until the intellect has examined the matter. For knowledge of the truth about such things seems to belong to the mind alone, not to the combination of mind and body."[169] The use of the senses for speculative ends, and therefore the theory of their role in one's knowledge (which is theorized in Aristotle), is the product of the propensity "of misusing the order of nature. For the proper purpose of the sensory perceptions given me by nature is simply to inform the mind of what is beneficial or harmful for the

168 Ibid., 56.
169 Ibid., 57.

composite of which the mind is a part; and to this extent they are sufficiently clear and distinct. But I misuse them by treating them as reliable touchstones for immediate judgments about the essential nature of the bodies located outside us; yet this is an area where they provide only very obscure information."[170] Therefore, the practical end of the substantial union adequately answers the objection to divine truthfulness and counters the argument in favor of an empiricism built on this very union.

6.5. *The Errors of Nature*

In general, the foundation of science upon divine truthfulness bears an optimistic vision of nature and its teachings. "Indeed, there is no doubt that everything that I am taught by nature contains some truth."[171] Error is something acquired and so can always be eliminated. It is unnatural, you might say. Perhaps the most telling passage of divine truthfulness and the Cartesian vision of nature is a paragraph in the *Principles* wherein Descartes analyzes how the prejudices regarding the nature of bodies are formed. A newborn has a spontaneous mechanistic vision of the world. In early childhood, or first childhood, there is no attribution of colors, sounds, and smells to external objects that fill the mind. On the contrary, "size, figures, and movements" do not appear to the newborn as simple mental states, "rather, (...) things, or (...) properties of certain things, that (...) seem to exist, or at least can exist, outside of himself." Prejudices come later, in later or second childhood, and it is quite the task to remove them. But the newly born enters into the world, literally born to the truth and spontaneously distinguishes between what is purely sensation and what can actually be something, or exist outside the mind.[172] The battle against the prejudices picked up in childhood is never a battle against nature, and this optimistic vision of nature

170 Ibid., 57–58.
171 Ibid., 56.
172 Cf. *Principles of Philosophy*, I, § 71. *The Philosophical Writings of Descartes, Volume I,* John Cottingham, *et al.*

provides the solution to the natural union of the body and soul as well. This, too, contains a message of truth, although here it is purely on the plane of the practical.

Nonetheless, the theory that states that the union of the body and soul has a practical end and so, on this plane, the feelings that the body provokes in the mind are true, leads to a residual problem. It is the final obstacle on the way to the foundation of science. Yes, it is still, always, about the foundation of science. Divine truthfulness guarantees clear and distinct ideas. God is not responsible for speculative error because this error can always be corrected. Neither can God be accused of having made things more difficult for men in their pursuit of the truth, for the intention behind the union of body and soul is a practical end. One notes that in these passages it is always about removing the obstacles to divine truthfulness, the real cornerstone to the foundation of science. But this construction risks collapsing at a final pitfall: if all this is true, feelings and compulsions would always be, practically speaking, true, and they would never move us in irresistible ways towards objectives that later reveal themselves to be harmful to the mind-body composite. And yet these cases arise. For example, there are illnesses that present themselves in desire, so as for the sake of one's own satisfaction actually undermine the subject's health. Take the case of dropsy, where the ill subject has an irresistible desire to drink even though to drink is poisonous to one's health. But if the practical fallacy of the senses cannot be corrected, then God is made out to be a deceiver. If God is a deceiver, the necessary assent of the knowing subject is no longer a mark of the truth, and if this is no longer a mark of the truth, then human science will have no guarantee that it really is speaking about the world. With this last remaining pitfall, seemingly marginal, what is at stake is no less than the cohesiveness of the whole complex construction of science built up to this point. Again, as in the fourth meditation, all that which is demonstrated of divine truthfulness and the guarantee it offers science can all be ruinously turned on its head by a single fact—error. We see theoretical error in the fourth meditation, and practical error in the sixth, and if this error cannot be reconciled with divine truthfulness, one is forced to renounce the guarantee of science for anything he believes to have demonstrated up to this point.

The answer to this last difficulty is surprising. Essentially, Descartes admits that there are some cases that ought to be considered true and proper "errors" of nature, of the same nature that a few pages back he declares to always be truthful. This time, faced with the irresistible urges of the subject suffering from dropsy, Descartes abandons the road traditionally taken in the fourth meditation, or the way that resolves the problem of evil by bringing the focus back to man's limited perspective. The difference between the fourth and sixth meditations could not be greater. In the fourth meditation God realizes his end *because of* the presence of error in the world, and so what we call evil does not actually appear as such to the divine perspective. In the sixth meditation, however, God does not always reach the foreseen goal, and so when these cases come up they are "true errors" of nature. Even for God, in this case of dropsy the thirst of the subject is real evil.

In the fourth meditation, Descartes is able to proceed along the traditional lines of the compatibility of the ends of God with what to human eyes appears to be evil in that the realization of the hypothesized end, the creation of the best world, was absolutely beyond verification by the finite intellect. Now Descartes is forced to admit the reality of evil because of the practical end that he has to hypothesize in describing the substantial union of the body and the soul and the fact that it can be verified. It is easy for anyone to verify whether the satisfaction of some irresistible desire is dangerous for some organism or not. The solution to this problem cannot revert back, then, to a vision that is above and beyond the reach of the human mind: even if man could gain access to the divine mind, the thirst of the patient suffering from dropsy is still an evil. How can divine truthfulness be reconciled to this new obstacle? Well, according to Descartes, God is not guilty in these cases, either. Hence, his truthfulness is preserved, for God could not have done otherwise—once the human machine is set in motion, with all the laws that regulate the transmission of the impulses in the nerves from one's periphery to one's brain, and once it is established that a certain sensation in the mind corresponds with a certain movement provoked in the brain, God can no longer modify his decisions. His immutability, this time in conflict with his truthfulness, prevents him from doing so. All that God can do to accomplish the goal of guaranteeing what is best with respect to the well-being of mankind God has already done. He has decided that the soul experience a certain feeling in the event of a certain corporeal change, and he has decided to locate this feeling in the part of the body where, in the majority of cases, it is most useful for the conservation of the mind-body composite that it be made known. But once he makes his decision, it is no longer possible to change it, and when the body is not well disposed, the feeling that the mind experiences and the presence of that feeling in the part of the body where it is normally most useful that it be located inflict harm rather than benefit to the composite.

The drama surrounding this conclusion deserves to be emphasized, despite Descartes' resolute satisfaction. He thinks that this problem can be considered resolved by the simple fact that, speaking in percentages, the cases that contrast with the practical end of the mind-body union are very few. For the first time in the history of rational theology of Christian inspiration, a philosopher admits that the evil man experiences in nature is not due to the limited vision of the human mind. Nor is it an error of perspective that would disappear if one could observe the world through God's eyes. Rather, it is a real evil that appears as such even to God in that it violates his own intentions. Descartes comes to this conclusion because he must hypothesize a practical end for the mind-body union that is verifiable even for the human mind. Moreover, he has to hypothesize a practical end of the mind-body union in order to salvage divine truthfulness from the accusation of having thought up a kind of union of the body and soul that favors speculative error. He has to hypothesize this practical end, then, to found the truth of science. Evil enters into the theoretical universe in modern metaphysics as a residual consequence of the attempt to construct science on a positive vision of nature, and of the relationship God has with the world. Faced with this consequence, the infinitely powerful Cartesian God is absolved only because something has kept him from reaching his end—his own immutability.

Chapter Four
The Fate of the Work

"René Descartes is a hero. He started over from the beginning and has only now restored philosophy to its proper place after the passing of thousands of years."[1] The idea of an epic rupture out of which Descartes initiates the thought of modern philosophy, which Hegel makes his own with these lines, is by now part of the self-identity of contemporary philosophy.

It would not be improper to say that there is a sense in which the fate of Cartesian metaphysics coincides with the most significant developments in philosophy even in our own day. From Descartes' *Metaphysical Meditations* idealism and phenomenology were born. In opposition to Descartes, or through a critique of his work, modern empiricism and hermeneutics emerged. More generally, the terms set down by Descartes for philosophers are still alive in the philosophical debates of the twentieth century. Moore, Austin, and Wittgenstein[2] discuss skepticism with incessant references to Descartes. At the heart of Russell's[3] theory of knowledge there is the search for an undeniable foundation of

1   G. W. F. Hegel, *Lectures on the History of Philosophy, Volume III.* E. S. Haldane and Frances H. Simpson, trans. (University of Nebraska Press, 1995).
2   In particular, see G. I. Moore, *Some Main Problems of Philosophy* (George Allen & Unwin, 1962) and *Philosophical Papers* (Oxford University Press in three editions, 1990); J. L. Austin, *Sense and Sensibilia* (Oxford University Press, 1962); L. Wittgenstein, *Über Gewissheit, On Certainty* (Wiley-Blackwell, 1991); B. Russell, *Skeptical Essays* (Routledge, 2004), and *Selected Papers of Bertrand Russell* (The Modern Library, 1955).
3   B. Russell, *The Problems of Philosophy* (Simon & Brown, 2013).

knowledge. The debate surrounding the mind and body of contemporary analytic philosophy is built up around explicit references and opposition to Cartesian dualism.[4] Chomsky's linguistics is structured around a reinterpretation of inneism in Descartes.[5]

In a more localized sense, the fate of the *Meditations* coincides with the hegemony that Descartes' thought poses to the philosophical discussion of the second half of the sixteen-hundreds, a period which is not wrongly dubbed the "Cartesian Age," with the particular tone of metaphysical reflection that was maintained until the arrival of Kant. Descartes' metaphysics was by definition more successful that his physics, even though physics is the science that metaphysics is called upon on to establish. The terms that mark the metaphysical conversation during the Cartesian Era are the following: the foundation of knowledge on the subject, the nature of the subject and the doctrine of ideas, the possibility of knowing the essence of God and the proof of his existence, and the separation of the mind from the body and substantial union.

Even if Descartes was frustrated in his attempts to replace the teachings of Aristotle in the universities with his own philosophy, it is nonetheless true that an enormous section of academic culture has been marked by the discussions of this new philosophy. While Descartes was still alive, the Dutch universities were split as to whether or not to accept his philosophy. The University of Utrecht was vehemently opposed, though it did not lack a healthy number

4   In the paper, "Self, Mind and Body" in *Freedom and Resentment and Other Essays*, (London, 1974), P. F. Strawson describes Cartesian dualism as a position that bestows "a persuasive form and lasting influence on one of the most fundamental conceptual errors that the human mind is inclined to harbor, having to do with the basic categories of thought." An outline of the polemical confrontation with Descartes in the great debate of the nineteen-hundreds regarding the notion of the human mind can be read in G. Ryle's *Concept of the Mind* (University of Chicago Press, 2002). More on this debate can be read in M. Di Francesco's *Introduzione alla filosofia della mente* (Rome: Carocci, 1996).

5   Cf. N. Chomsky, *Cartesian Linguistics: A Chapter in the History of Rationalist Thought* (Cambridge University Press, 2009).

of "Cartesian" professors, while the universities at Leiden and Franeker were more open if not decidedly in favor. At the Leuven in Belgium, Arnold Geulincx emerged as the interpreter of the new metaphysics. In Germany the most illustrious Cartesian was Clauberg, first a professor at Herborn and then at Duisburg. The Protestant academics in Geneva assumed many of the Cartesian terms, starting with Jean-Robert Chouet and later with Jean Leclerc. It is within these universities in Holland and Germany that true and proper commentaries on the *Meditations* were produced, evidence of the intention to make it into a text for philosophical formation.[6]

In England, it was at Cambridge that the Platonism of Descartes found favor. The *Meditations* were not translated into English until 1680 by William Molineux, but the Latin draft of the *Meditations* enjoyed rapid diffusion. The *Discourse*, however, containing Descartes' thought on metaphysics had already been translated into English in 1649. Before decidedly breaking with Cartesian metaphysics, Henry More had announced that it had won him over and adopted much of Descartes' arguments for inneism, immortality of the soul, and the *a priori* demonstration of the existence of God. He was followed by Edward Stillingfleet and Ralph Cudworth. The case of Stillingfleet and Cudworth is

6   J. Clauberg, *Paraphrasis in renati Des Cartes Meditationes de prima philosophia*. Duisburgi ad Rhenum 1658; L. Schotanus, *Exegesis in primam et secundam meditationem R. Cartesii* (Franequerae 1687); L. van Velthuysen, *De initiis primae philosophiae, juxta fundamenta clarissimi Cartesii tradita in ipsius Meditationibus nec non de Deo et mente humana* (Trajecti ad Rhenum 1662); C. Wittich, *Annotationes ad Renati des Cartes Meditationes* (Dordrecht 1688); J. L. Wolzogen, *Annotationes ad meditationes metaphysicas Renati Des Cartes*, 1657, but later in the *Bibliotheca fratrum polonorum*, Irenopoli, post annum 1656, vol. II. Regarding the integration of Cartesian thought in Holland, see Thomas Verbeek's *Descartes and the Dutch: Early Reaction to Cartesian Philosophy 1637–1650* (Carbondale and Edwardsville, 1992). On Cartesian thought in Germany, see F. Trevisani's *Descartes in Germania* (Milan: FrancoAngeli, 1992).

interesting. They were quite worried, as More initially was not, about the potentially atheistic aspects of the mechanisms in Cartesian physics, though fully convinced of the validity of the proofs Descartes laid out for the existence of God.[7] The introduction of Cartesian metaphysics in England was at first so enthusiastic that it won over even those who would later become its greatest adversaries. Such is the case with Walter Charleton, Gassendi's disciple and champion of Epicureanism. He opened his *Darkness of Atheism Dispelled by the Lights of Nature* by paraphrasing Descartes' proof for the existence of God in the third meditation.[8] It was not until John Locke and his *Essay Concerning Human Understanding* in 1690 that we see these developments seriously countered. The attack on Cartesian inneism, the *a priori* proof for the existence of God, and even Locke's mildly developed theory, which nevertheless fostered great dialogue, about God being able to make matter think, all contributed to a strong counter-front to the Cartesian system. In British territories, however, the discussion of Cartesian metaphysics once again gained momentum due to the enormous

7   Cf. H. More's *Antidotus adversus Atheismum* (London 1652). In chapter eight there is another attempt at the *a priori* proof of the existence of God. See also *Immortalitas Animae* (London 1659); E. Stillingfleet in his *Origines sacrae* of 1662 defends the Cartesian *a priori* proof, and Ralph Cudworth in his *True Intellectual System of the Universe* (London 1678) proposes an elaborate formulation of this argument. See the edition printed in 1977 (New York, Hildesheim), 722ff. This was reprinted in 1977 by Hildesheim-New York. The defense of the *a priori* argument is essential to the theological rationalism of Samuel Clark. See *A Discourse Concerning the Being and Attributes of God* (London 1705). More generally, on the early influence of Descartes in England, see A. Pacchi's *Caresio in Inghilterra* (Rome-Bari: Laterza, 1973); Brunello Lotti, *L'iperbole del dubbio. Lo scetticismo cartesiano nella filosofia inglese tra Sei e Settecento* (Firenze: Le Lettere, 2010); Paola Dessì and Brunello Lotti, *Eredità cartesiane nella cultura Britannica* (Firenze: Le Lettere, 2011).

8   W. Charleton, *The Darkness of Atheism Dispelled By the Lights of Nature* (London 1652), 6–21.

success of Malebranche's presentation of Descartes' thought. The success of Malebranche's work, in a Platonic environment already somewhat open to Cartesian philosophy as Cambridge was, is understandable in that Malebranche (and despite his refutation of inneism) praised the Cartesian Platonism stressing the reality of the essences of things outside the mind. The *Recherche de la vérité* was translated twice into English in 1694, and Malebranche's idealistic version of Cartesian thought was reproduced word for word in John Norris' *Essay Towards the Theory of the Ideal or Intelligible Word*, which was edited sometime between 1701 and 1704.

Barred from the universities on account of the placement of his work on the List of Prohibited Books in 1663, Cartesian metaphysics saw great success in French culture, and it is in Malebranche that we find most tension and most fidelity to the original Cartesian metaphysics. In the last quarter-century the great post-Cartesian metaphysical contributions of Spinoza, Malebranche, and Leibniz were responsible for the development of the Cartesian metaphysical categories as the main points of reference for all philosophical discussion.[9]

1. *God*

The individual terms of Cartesian metaphysics have a life of their own, one might say, even apart from the original system. During the Cartesian Era, the project of establishing a science such as the one elaborated by Descartes through his metaphysics was forgotten. In Descartes' metaphysical foundation of the sciences, there was always the possibility of coming to the truth without direct contact with the divine mind. Abandoning this project is a result

---

9   P. S. Régis' *Système de philosophie, concernant la logique, la métaphysique, la physique et la morale* (Lyon 1691) is largely a reprisal of Descartes in light of Malebranche's philosophical contribution. There is also the *Méditations sur la métaphysique* (Lanion 1678), a work which unfolds like a reproduction of the *Meditations*, although ripe with Malebranche's influence.

of the renunciation of the theory that allowed the incommensurability of the human and divine mind, or the free creation of eternal truths, a doctrine that all post-Cartesian philosophers had recognized, either implicitly, or explicitly as the heart of Cartesian metaphysics. This same theory is challenged in the great post-Cartesian metaphysicians where there is the strongest echo of Descartes, like Malebranche and Spinoza, as well as in those metaphysicians farthest from and most critical of Descartes, like Leibniz. Yet there are nuances among these three cases. Malebranche and Leibniz refute the theological premise from which Descartes deduces the theory of the free creation of eternal truths, the primacy of the infinite potency in God. Both opt for a divine will and potency limited by the content of the intellect. What is possible imposes itself on the divine will and power, and God in return cannot do but what is possible, what his intellect shows him. According to Leibniz, "necessary truths are founded on the principle of non-contradiction and the possibility or impossibility of the essences themselves, and in these matters one does not consider of the free will of God."[10] For a Cartesian who wanted to always put himself forward, Malebranche has a very provocative refutation of infinite divine power. "His wisdom renders him (God), so to speak, *impotent.*"[11] Spinoza came up with his own approach, for contrary to Malebranche he takes up the privilege of divine potency and deduces from this the dependence of both existence and the essences of things on the divine essence. "Not only is God the efficient cause of existence, but of the essences of things as well."[12] But Spinoza rejects the Cartesian theory of absolute divine liberty both with respect to existence as well as produced essences. Descartes affirms against tradition that inasmuch as God is free to create the existence of things, regarding the essences of these things he is also free. Spinoza shatters

---

10   G. W. Leibniz, *Discourse on Metaphysics* (Hackett Publishing Company, 1991), § 13.

11   N. Malebranche, *Traité de la nature et de la grâce.* I, XXXVIII. Emphasis mine.

12   B. Spinoza, *Ethica* (Penguin Classics, 2005), I, proposition XXV.

Cartesian reasoning beginning with Descartes' own presuppositions, and he begins with Descartes' theory of essence and existence both being equally dependent on God. For as God is not free with respect to the production of essences, so he is neither free in the production of existence, even though both indeed depend on God. Actually, Spinoza considers the freedom of indifference that Descartes concedes to God "a terrific obstacle to science."[13] In each of the three systems, the eternal truths could not have been different than they are, therefore when the human mind has access to these nothing further is needed to guarantee this knowledge. There is no room for doubt as to the truth of clear and distinct ideas. "He who has a true idea likewise knows that he has it and cannot doubt the truth of the thing."[14]

As a result of abandoning the necessity of guaranteeing the indubitable, the centrality of the subject in the foundation of science is also lost. As much as Cartesian metaphysics absorbs God into the realm of finite knowledge, so much do the post-Cartesian metaphysicians (most notably in Malebranche and Spinoza) move the foundation of knowledge along a different route, focusing instead on God and the infinite. Malebranche maintains that we do not have a clear and distinct idea of the mind. The internal sense, the Cartesian consciousness, is even opposed to clear and distinct knowledge. "Such is not the case with the soul, [which] we do not know through its idea—we do not see it in God; we know it only through *consciousness,* and because of this, our knowledge of it is imperfect. Our knowledge of our soul is limited to what we sense taking place in us."[15] Instead, the infinite is constantly present to the mind. Spinoza's *Ethics* starts off with the demonstration of the existence of one singular substance—God. The finite mind, like all finite beings, consequently loses the character of substance attributed to it by Descartes. They are made

13 Ibid., proposition XXXIII, s. II.
14 Ibid., proposition XLIII.
15 N. Malebranche, *The Search After Truth* (Cambridge University Press: Cambridge, 1997), 237.

into a mode of that one singular substance. Through this de-substantialization of the finite, Spinoza builds the most sensational case for the centralization of the infinite in the post-Cartesian climate. Here there is the absorption of the finite into the infinite.

Nonetheless, in both Spinoza and Malebranche the centrality of the infinite is possible according to a choice Descartes made in his metaphysics, above all in the theory crucial to the *Meditations* which states that knowledge of the infinite is positive on the part of the human mind. It is precisely the acceptance of this central point of the Cartesian metaphysics that places the infinite at the center of the system, joined by the rejection of the abyss between the finite and infinite that was set forth by Cartesian metaphysics in the creation of eternal truths. In a Cartesianesque manner, Malebranche affirms, "not only does the mind have an idea of the infinite, it even has it even before that of the finite."[16] Malebranche tries to keep knowledge of God and his incomprehensibility united, as does Descartes, but Spinoza expresses his opinion without restraint on the matter and concedes to the finite mind exactly that knowledge which is adequate in what concerns God. Instead in Descartes, it is not possible to know that we have reached adequate knowledge even in the case of knowledge of finite entities. Spinoza writes, "the human mind has adequate knowledge of the eternal and infinite essence of God."[17]

Ignorance of the essence of God is Thomas Aquinas' first line in arguing the impossibility of demonstrating *a priori* the existence of God. In fact, as he says, this demonstration would have to use the real definition of the essence of God as its major premise. Thomas only admits any demonstration beginning with finite effects, that is, the *a posteriori* demonstration. But Descartes, on one hand, obtains a clear and distinct idea of God from the human mind, and on the other rejects every attempt to demonstrate the existence of God that does not use knowledge of his nature. The three major post-Cartesian metaphysicians, Malebranche,

16   Ibid., 232.
17   B. Spinoza, *Ethica*. II, proposition XLVII.

Spinoza, and Leibniz, all move along the key presupposition of knowledge of the infinite in the Cartesian system, and all three draw the possibility of demonstrating the existence of God starting from the knowledge of his essence. The centrality of the *a priori* proof surrounding the existence of God was born in this context. This proof, which Aquinas includes in the part of Anselm's thesis that he rejects, was left standing as the monarch over all demonstrations of God's existence. The success of the *a priori* proof for the existence of God was such that it provoked lively discussion even beyond the metaphysical, and bled into the great European philosophical journals of the day. "Behold a debate that is becoming fashionable," it was heard said to a participant at a debate.[18]

British culture, thanks to Lockean Empiricism and the momentum of finalism due to the growing success of Newtonian physics, was devoted to the *a posteriori* proofs. Nonetheless, the sense of the critique of Descartes' proofs beginning with finite effects, each one incapable of demonstrating the infinity of God, is present in the theological rationalism of Samuel Clarke, and above all in the elegant pages of the *Dialogues Concerning Natural Religion* of David Hume.

Kant came to the scene in the wake of this modern buzz around the *a priori* proof. He dedicated part of the *Transcendental Dialectics* to an assessment of the state of rational theology. He gives an account of the Cartesian Age, noting how the *a priori* proof is the only one that can ever hope to demonstrate that an infinitely perfect God exists. Nonetheless, the inevitable

18 This is a reference to Desmaizeaux, in the "Nouvelles de la République des Lettres" of November 1701. The "Histoire des ouvrages des scavans," the "Journal des Savants," the "Journal de Trevoux," and the "Nouvelles de la République des Lettres," between 1700 and 1703 all granted space to the lively debate regarding the *a priori* proof. It was a debate that included, among others, even Leibniz. On this point, see A. C. Kors' *Atheism in France 1650-1729: Volume I, The Orthodox Sources of Disbelief* (Princeton 1990), 334–75.

advantage that he grants the *a priori* proof also marks the obvious weakness of rational theology in general. When this proof is cut down, thus collapses the whole castle of rational theology—and to undermine the *a priori* proof is a very easy task, according to Kant, due to its intrinsic weaknesses. Paradoxically, Cartesian theological rationalism has been a decisive step towards the confutation of the whole of rational theology.

There is an insidious sense in which the Cartesian decision to render the divine nature completely intelligible seems to end up as a failure of theological reasoning—Descartes' brash non-apologetic and exclusively philosophical role attributed to God. Even during Descartes' own day, this use of theology led to the first accusations of atheism, largely by Gisbert Voët, which greatly saddened Descartes.[19] With his *Athei detecti,* the Jesuit Hardouin exposed the atheism implicit in the philosophical conception of God, and he gave a special place of honor for Descartes.[20] On the other hand, the obvious strangeness of the Cartesian God juxtaposed with the God of faith pushes Pascal to object to Descartes as "not useful and uncertain."[21] Despite the care Descartes gave to the maintenance of the incomprehensibility of God, the central theory of his metaphysics which holds that the mind possesses a clear and distinct idea of God, authorizes an merciless scrutiny (in light of reason) of the attributes of the Christian God. For this, rational theology ends up beaten and battered. Pierre Bayle dedicated a particular contribution to this dissection of the monotheistic God.[22] This modern defeat of rational theology, put through the sieve of Cartesian clear and distinct ideas, also fed Kant's abandoning hope of constructing a science around God, and in general the science of metaphysics.

19 On these matters, see Theo Verbeek, *René Descartes et Martin Schoock. La querrelle de Utrecht* (Paris 1988).
20 J. Hardouin, *Athei detecti.* In *Opera varia.* Amstelodami 1723.
21 B. Pascal, *Pensées,* § 887.
22 G. Cantelli appropriately entitled his work on Bayle *Teologia e ateismo* (Florence 1969).

2. Ideas

This great post-Cartesian metaphysics thereby abandons the foundation of knowledge of the world on the knowledge of one's self, and moves its attention on God and true knowledge that the mind has of God. Yet, the centrality of the subject in the foundation of science is only temporarily shelved. Hunted by the foundation of science, the thinking self comes back in play in post-Cartesian philosophy, and resurfaces in the conversation of idealism.[23]

"I think every one agrees," Malebranche says at the beginning of his examination of the nature and origin of ideas, "that we do not perceive objects external to us by themselves. We see the sun, the stars, and an infinity of objects external to us; and it is not likely that the soul should leave the body to stroll about the heavens, as it were, in order to behold all these objects. Thus, it does not see them by themselves, and out mind's immediate object when it sees the sun, for example, is not the sun, but something that is intimately joined to our soul, and this is what I call an *idea*."[24] Malebranche's affirmation, according to which everyone would be agreed in maintaining that in the knowledge of bodies we do not know the bodies themselves but the ideas of these bodies, would not have made sense within an Aristotelian or Thomistic empirical philosophy. On the inside of these theories of knowledge, ideas are *means* of knowledge of bodies, and not the *object* of knowledge. What Malebranche presents as obvious is the extreme character of Descartes' theory, which states that the immediate object of any perception is an idea. "I am taking the word 'idea' to refer to whatever is immediately perceived by the mind."[25] What one knows is the reality represented by the idea, or its objective reality. The difficulty that Descartes has in passing

---

23 Beyond the great revival of the foundation of knowledge on one's self in the nineteen-hundreds, it continues explicitly in E. Husserl's *Cartesian Meditations* (1931).

24 N. Malebranche, *The Search After Truth*, op. cit., 217.

25 "Replies to the Third Set of Objections," in *The Philosophical Writings of Descartes Volume II*, John Cottingham, *et al.*, 127.

from mental states to the external world becomes a simple impossibility for Malebranche. Ideas no longer mediate between the mind and the objects represented, but are themselves objects of knowledge. Hence they do not in any way give witness to the existence of an external world. He writes, "on the supposition that the world is destroyed and that God nonetheless produces the same traces in our brain, or rather that He presents to our mind the same ideas that are produced in the presence of objects, we would see the same beauties...By itself your room is absolutely invisible.... I contend that Chinese people who have never been here can see in their country everything I see when I look at your room, assuming—what is not at all impossible—that their brains are agitated in the same way as mine when I consider it.... You seem to me to have trouble enough distinguishing ideas, which alone are visible by themselves, from the objects they represent, which are invisible to the mind because they can neither act on it nor represent themselves to it."[26] The Cartesian theory of ideas poses something new to the ancient philosophical problem, having to do with the possibility of verifying the existence of the external world.[27]

To understand the progress of the post-Cartesian idealistic trend, it is helpful to go back in memory to Descartes' doctrine of ideas. In the proper sense ideas are what represent things that can exist outside of the mind. False ideas are what represent the quality of things that cannot exist outside the mind. They are mental states only, even though it seems they make reference to something existing outside the mind. Instead, in a broader sense, all mental states, including materially false ideas, are ideas. The choice

26 N. Malebranche, *Dialogues on Metaphysics and Religion* (Cambridge University Press, 1997), 11–12.
27 Yet this is an eternal question in philosophy. It is surprising how like the passage from Malebranche cited above is to well noted passage of H. Putnam wherein Putnam states that the human brain, conserved in a solution and given electrical stimulation, would have the same experiences that a human being experiences through the course of his life. Cf. H. Putnam, *Reason, Truth, and History* (Cambridge University Press, 1981).

Malebranche made was to exclude mental states that do not denote anything that can exist outside the mind from the realm of ideas. If they are not ideas in the proper sense, on the whole these mental states are not ideas. They are sentiments or feelings, perceptions that can only be traced back to the perceiving subject.

On the other hand, ideas in a proper sense are ideas because they represent something that has reality even outside the mind, and hence it is this reality and not the perception that the mind has of it that merits the name idea. For the essences that render ideas "true" are independent from thought, they are not in the mind. And since these essences were not freely created by God (as we know, Malebranche rejects the theory of the free creation of essences) they are a part of his nature. To have ideas, then, is the same as saying that one sees the essences of things in God. Malebranche's idealism was born from the fusion of two Cartesian theories: the theory of ideas and the reality of essences (in this case, the mathematical characteristics of bodies), and the subjectivity of secondary qualities of the bodies themselves. The human mind only knows the essences of things, and these essences are independent from the mind and external to it—the essences are in God. Since the essences of things in no way indicate the existence of these things, knowledge of bodies (of what are bodies) cannot vouch for their existence. Perceptions of the qualities of objects are only in the mind, but these do not in themselves trace back to anything outside the subject, as Descartes has already stated. It follows that neither true ideas (essences of things) nor the perceptions of the mind make reference to the external world. As to the theological argument Descartes used to guarantee the natural propensity to believe in the existence of bodies outside the mind, Malebranche rejected this in that the divine guarantee can only extend itself to clear and distinct ideas.

Malebranche's idealism was attacked right away by Antoine Arnauld in the name of Cartesian orthodoxy in his *Des vraies et das fausses idées* in 1683. Even Arnauld underlined an undeniably Cartesian aspect of ideas—their capacity to represent something (ideas as modes of thoughts). But according to Arnauld, what an idea represents is the object itself existing outside the mind. For him, perceptions are enough to explain this capacity to represent something external to the mind, and it is not necessary to hypothesize about a being distinct from both the modes of the mind and external bodies, as in Malebranche's idea. There is no doubt that in both Malebranche and Arnauld something of the original Cartesian theory is stirred up (in Arnauld, ideas as modes of the mind; and in Malebranche, the objective reality of ideas), yet it is the idealistic interpretation, even if not necessarily the version by Malebranche, that was destined to become the lasting banner of the Cartesian theory of ideas. In the meantime, Arnauld's "realistic" attempt of an interpretation is left out as of minor importance, before being recovered by Thomas Reid who used it against the widespread idealistic developments of the theory of Cartesian knowledge.[28]

Among the many Cartesian paradoxes of Malebranche, one must keep in mind that despite all his opposition to Descartes' inneism, Malebranche is still a full heir to Cartesian rationalism against empiricism. Idealism in Malebranche hinges on the representative content of what Descartes calls innate ideas, mathematical essences, independent of the mind and their manifestations. He makes a stark distinction between these ideas and adventitious ones that are purely perceptions of the mind. Though proceeding within a theory of ideas of Cartesian origin, if one does not accept this aspect of Cartesian rationalism he or she ends up with Berkeley's idealism. Berkeley is of inverted symmetry with Malebranche, withdrawing his concession of an ontological distinction between the primary and secondary qualities of represented things. All the characteristics of objects, both the mathematical characteristics and the qualities, are purely representations of the mind and they are what make up the object of knowledge.

The result is always the same. Ideas are no longer instruments that represent objects external to the mind, but are instead obstacles between the mind and the external world, whether or not Cartesian

28   Thomas Reid. *Essays on the Intellectual Powers of Man* (Edinburgh 1785).

ideas bind themselves to the reality of essences (true ideas in Cartesian memory), or bind themselves to the rejection of reality outside the mind of what is represented (all ideas are "materially false," as Descartes says, they are only perceptions of the mind); or whether the balance of Cartesian ideas is upset in favor of the mind's representative modes, or the balance is upset in favor of the objective reality of an idea. "I do not see what reason might induce me to believe, on the basis of what we perceive, in the existence of bodies outside the mind," writes Berkeley, "I say it is recognized by everyone (and it is proven by what happens in dreams, and likewise in madness) that it would be possible that we received all the ideas that we have now even if there were no bodies existing outside of what looks like them. It is thereby evident that the hypothesis of external bodies is not necessary for the generation of our ideas."[29]

Descartes rolled out a new map of the mental universe. It was for Aristotelians intellectual activity that was properly called spiritual—this is what distinguished the mind from matter. For Descartes thought and ideas constituted conscious activity, even sensations and feelings. This revision of the mental map is taken up by Descartes' opponents as well. Locke, for example, speaks of "that awareness that is inseparable from thought, and for as I can tell, it is essential to it—it is impossible for anyone to perceive without *perceiving* that he is perceiving."[30] Consequently, an idea, for Locke as for Descartes, is "whatever thing that occupies our mind when the mind is thinking."[31]

---

29 G. Berkeley, *Treatise Concerning the Principles of Human Knowledge*, § 18.

30 J. Locke, *An Essay Concerning Human Understanding* (Oxford University Press, 1979), II. XXVII, 11, II. Emphasis mine.

31 Ibid. The conscience, as the characterizing activity of the mind, is on the whole an element that continues to be emphasized in the contemporary debate regarding the mind, as a strong objection against materialistic opposition to Descartes. There are many opposed to the reductionism in the argument surrounding the human mind. Cf. Thomas Nagle's "What Is It Like To Be a Bat?" *The Philosophical Review.* LXXXIII, 4 (October 1974): 435–50.

The difficulty of putting oneself in contact with the external world starting from ideas is set in motion by Descartes' theory of knowledge, and touches empiricism as well. In this case the difficulty is shown to be a revival of the skeptical arguments resurrected by Descartes in the first meditation. It was mentioned prior how Berkeley used the experience of a dream (as in the first meditation) against the inference of an external world when starting from ideas. In the *Critique de la Recherche de la Vérité* of 1675, and the *nouvelle Dissertation sur la Recherche de la Vérité* in 1979, Foucher explicitly linked the Cartesian concept of ideas to the impossibility of knowing the external bodies as argued by Skeptics. The impossibility of proving that an external world exists by using one's own perceptions is explicitly stated by David Hume to be a reprisal of the Skeptical reflection.[32]

Implicit recognition of the affiliation between Berkeley's idealism and Descartes appeared in a chapter of the first edition of Kant's *Critique of Pure Reason,* though it was taken out in the second edition. "The transcendental idealist can be a empirical realist (...) that is, can concede the existence of matter without straying from the simple consciousness of oneself, and admit something more than the certainty of the representations in me, more than the *cogito ergo sum.*"[33] That is to say that the *cogito* is the point of departure in Kantian idealism, but not where one ends (as is the case with Berkeley). Nonetheless, the "empirical realism" that Kant sets up against Berkeley's idealism allows that there are things that exist outside the mind, though what this reality is in itself is never accessible to the human mind. In fact, experience is a mental construction accomplished through something that is innate to it—not Cartesian ideas, but through the functions that make up the content of thought, the *a priori* forms of the intuition and the intellect.

32 Cf. D. Hume. *Treatise on Human Nature* (Oxford University Press, 2000), I, IV.
33 I. Kant. *Kritik der reinen Vernuft* in *Werke* (Wissenschafltiche Buchgesellscaft: Darmstadt, 1983). Vol. 4, 2; page 276 (A 370).

Although Kantian inneism (surrounding the functions of the mind) does not bear any likeness to the inneism found in Descartes (here, an inneism regarding the content of the mind), the role inneism plays is analogous in the two thinkers, for even in Kant inneism is utilized to justify the organization of experience based on Descartes' model of how innate ideas function with regard to the knowledge of bodies. The principal organizer of experience is decidedly shifted from the world to the self, a self that contrary to the subject in Cartesian thought is not a substance but an organizing principle of all the activities of the mind. One has knowledge of one's self only when on the inside of its operations, as it is not possible to make it the direct object of investigation nor, precisely as Descartes claims, a favored object of knowledge. The "Copernican Revolution" that Kant claimed to have accomplished, the inversion of the center of knowledge from the external world to the subject, is the spawn of the revolution that Descartes was responsible for when he placed the subject at the center of knowledge. "Descartes, like Fichte after him, takes steps from his own self as if from that which is most certain (...) just like that, philosophy is in one fell swoop transferred to a totally new territory and point of view—into the sphere of subjectivity."[34] In post-Cartesian metaphysical undertakings the self is lost and the centering point of the system becomes God, but in the theories of knowledge the self reigns yet.[35]

34 G. W. F. Hegel, *Lectures the History of Philosophy,* III.2.
35 The claim that metaphysics focuses on the self, one's self, and that this is the characteristic of post-Cartesian philosophy, has been declared by Heidegger in his reconstruction of the history of metaphysics. According to Heidegger, a focus on the subject in Cartesian philosophy constitutes the fulfillment of Western metaphysics: certain knowledge substitutes the question of the being of that which exists. All metaphysics that comes after is intelligible through this inversion of the metaphysical question. From Leibniz's monad (which is the basis for the interpretation of all beings and even those not human beginning with the *ego,* for each monad apprehends the world and relates to it through its apprehensions), until Hegel for whom the *ego* is an absolute substance. Heidegger's is an interpre-

3. The Mind and the Body

Descartes' proposed heterogeneity between the mind and body immediately opened up the problem of justifying their reciprocal action. Descartes declared this to be a pseudo-problem not just because internal experience clearly gives witness to the fact of reciprocal action between the mind and body, but also because these difficulties can only arise from a false presupposition. "But I will say, for your benefit at least, that the whole problem contained in such questions arises simply from a supposition that is false and cannot in any way be proved, namely that, if the soul and the body are two different substances whose nature is different, this prevents them from being able to act on each other. And yet, those who admit the existence of real accidents like heat, weight and so on, have no doubt that these accidents can act on the body; but there is much more of a difference between them and it, i.e., between accidents and a substance, than there is between two substances."[36] But the calm that Descartes flaunted in this problem, above all in his confrontations with Gassendi, was not shared in the larger Cartesian school. Herein the theory of the heterogeneity between the mind and body was largely accepted, but there was also a sense of grave difficulty in this. Who really does one understand the interaction? One initial, radical solution was offered by occasionalism, or the doctrine that holds that finite beings are not the true causes of events, rather are only occasions for the intervention of the singular being bestowed with causal power—God.[37]

tation of the history of metaphysics as a progressive move away from the "to be." Descartes' interpretation is spread through many of Heidegger's works. There is a brief yet comprehensive presentation of this in J. L. Marion's "Heidegger et la situation métaphysique de Descartes," in *Archives de philosophie,*" 38 (1975), 253–65.

36   "Replies to the Fifth Set of Objections," in *The Philosophical Writings of Descartes Volume II,* John Cottingham, *et al.,* 275–276.
37   This comes up under various titles in the Occasionalists J. Clauberg (*Conjonction du corps et de l'âme en l'homme,* 1664), L. de la

Nevertheless, if occasionalism presented itself as a good way of explaining the regularity of succession in psychological and physical events, despite the absence of causality between the mind and the body, the difficulty in understanding the relation between the two heterogeneous substances that make up human nature is not, properly speaking, at the origin of occasionalism. If anything, the impossibility of reciprocal action between the mind and the body is a crucial matter that should render one particularly keen on the impossibility of conceiving of, in general, the interaction between creatures. Occasionalism is the fruit of the interpretation of the relationship between God and creatures as continuous creation, theorized by Descartes in the third meditation. "For it is quite clear to anyone who attentively considers the nature of time," says Descartes, "that the same power and action are needed to preserve anything at each individual moment of its duration as would be required to create that new thing anew if it were not yet in existence."[38] Therefore, many "Cartesians" interpret this to mean that it is not the event prior that causes those subsequent to it, rather God who, on the occasion of a particular event presenting itself, actually causes the next event himself. This is true both of material events that follow mental events, as well as material events that follow other material events. "If I said that it is no longer as difficult to conceive of how the mind of man without being extended can move the body, and how the body, without being a spiritual thing, can act on the mind, as it is to conceive of how a body has the power to move itself, and communicate its motion to another body, I don't think many people would pay attention to me. Yet there is nothing truer than what I have just said." This was said by one of the first "Occasionalists," Louis de La Forge.[39]

Forge (*Traité de l'esprit de l'homme*, 1666), A. Geulincx, G. de Cordemoy (*Discernement de l'âme et du corps*, 1666; *Discours physique de la parole*, 1668), and above all in the works of N. Malebranche.

38   *The Philosophical Writings of Descartes Volume II*, John Cottingham, *et al.*, 33.

39   L. de la Forge, *Traité de l'espirit de l'homme* (Paris 1974), 235.

Occasionalism urges a new kind of attention to the relation between cause and effect. In the events we judge to be the cause of other events, we only see regular succession. Fire always comes before smoke, for example. But temporal relation is not enough to rationally found the instinctive belief of a causal power of the event that precedes the event that follows. The crisis of the relation between cause and effect that ensues in light of this analysis offers a solution to the difficulty in grasping the relationship between two heterogeneous substances like the mind and body. There is no causality between psychological and physical events, as there is no causality in any sequence of events. The regularity in any succession of events is due exclusively to the regularity of the intervention on the part of the singular cause—God. The solution offered by occasionalism to the mind-body relationship is, so to speak, a happy relapse into a more general dissolution of any link between a cause and its effect. Essentially, Malebranche founded occasionalism on a critique of reasons that led an attribution of ties between the cause and effect among events. "After what has been said, I do not think anyone can doubt that those who claim the mind can form its own ideas of objects are mistaken, since they attribute to the mind the power of creating, and even of creating wisely and with order, although it has no knowledge of what it does—which is inconceivable. But the cause of their error is that men can never fail to judge that a thing is the cause of a given effect when the two are conjoined, given that the true cause of the effect is unknown to them. This is why everyone concludes that a moving ball which strikes another is the true and principal cause of the motion it communicates to the other, and that the soul's will is the true and principal cause of movement in the arms, and other such prejudices—because it always happens that a ball moves when struck by another, that our arms move almost every time we want them to, and that we do not sensibly perceive what else could be the cause of these movements."[40] From

40   N. Malebranche, *The Search After Truth*, op. cit., 224.

Malebranche's analysis came David Hume's critique of the rational foundation of the relation between cause and effect.

In order that the problem of the relation between the mind and the body be marked as a primary and necessary problem, it is instead that the causality between finite beings be ascertained. This is why the true dramatization and anti-Cartesian solutions to the problem are beyond occasionalism, beyond any system that allows causality among homogeneous substances while simultaneously accepting the heterogeneity of the mind and body. The monism of the substance and the dualism of the attributes of thought and extension in Spinoza, as well as the pre-established harmony in Leibniz are attempts to answer the problem of how material and psychological events might correspond to each other in the context of the difficulty of grasping reciprocal causality. The correspondence of mental and material events is explained, according to Spinoza, by the fact that the attribute of thought translates into mental language the same message that appears under the form of material events in the body. Here the attribute of thought is an attribute of the same substance to which extension is attributed. Leibniz explained the correspondence between mind and matter through the original coordination of events by God. They do not, then, have reciprocal causal reality.

Dualism, advanced using Cartesian terminology like the radical heterogeneity of the mind and body, endured a fragrant season, but the sun was destined to set on this period that characterized the second half of the seventeenth century. However, this is a strange adventure in human thought, given that material monism, which is one of the theories that opposed and replaced Cartesian dualism, also sinks its anchor in Cartesian thought. Notwithstanding Descartes' struggle against Hobbes' materialism, his anti-Aristotelian elevation of matter to the place of substance—that is, to the same level as thought—was a strong support for modern materialism. Again, Descartes' attribution to matter all vital functions, which in Aristotelianism are proper only to the soul, constituted a strong argument in this same direction. A materialist of the seventeenth century, Julien Offroy de La

Mettrie,[41] says it well in his famous text entitled *The Machine Man* when he boasts his Cartesian lineage with the reference of his title to Descartes' "animal machine."

---

41 La Mettrie, Julien Offray de, *The Machine Man*. Translated from the French by the Marquiss D'Argens. Dublin 1749. Available through the Gale Group online, Eighteenth Century Collection.

Bibliography

Primary Texts

R. Descartes. *Meditationes de prima philosophia; Méditations métaphysiques,* in *Oeuvres de Descartes.* C. Adam and P. Tannery, eds. (Paris, nouvelle edition 1964–1974), vols. VII, IX–1.

John Cottingham, Robert Stoothoff, Dugald Murdoch. *The Philosophical Writings of Descartes, Vols. 1–3* (Cambridge: Cambridge University Press, 1984).

Anthony Kenny, ed. *Descartes: Philosophical Letters* (University of Minnesota Press, 1981).

Bibliographical Survey

G. Sebba. *Bibliographia cartesiana. A Critical Guide to the Descartes Literature* (The Hague, 1964).

V. Chappel and W. Doney. *Twenty-five Years of Descartes Scholarship: 1960–1984* (New York, 1987).

J.R. Armogathe and V. Carraud. *Bibliographie cartésienne (1990–1996),* (Lecce, 2003).

Post 1996, see *Bulletin cartésien* published every year from 1972 onwards in the "Archives de Philosophie." One can find the *Bulletin* online at http://www.cartesius.net/bulletin.html.

Critical Works

We are indebted to French scholars for a series of classical monographs that have marked modern research of Cartesian metaphysics. They include: F. Alquié, *La découverte métaphysique de l'homme chez Descartes* (Paris 1953); M. Gueroult. *Descartes selon l'ordre des raisons.* Two volumes (Paris 1953); R. Lefèvre. *La métaphysique de Descartes* (Paris 1959); H. Gouhier, *La pensée métaphysique de Descartes* (Paris 1962). And, despite the fact that it is not wholly centered on the *Meditations,* see J. Laporte's *La rationalisme de Descartes* (Paris 1945). Another formidable influence has been E. Gilson's commentary on the *Discours de la méthode* (Paris 1930).

In the sixties and seventies, the range of critical contributions surrounding the *Meditations* expanded well beyond France. In the English language we have L. J. Beck's *The Metaphysics of Descartes. A Study of the "Meditations"* (Oxford, 1967); A. Kenny's *Descartes. A Study of His Philosophy* (New York 1968); M.D. Wilson's *Descartes* (London 1978). H. G. Frankfurt is concise in his interpretation of the Cartesian project in widely read and debated *Demons, Dreamers and Madmen: The Defense of Reason in Descartes' Meditations* (Indianapolis-New York 1970). So is the work by H. Caton, *The Origin of Subjectivity* (New Haven, Connecticut, 1973). There is also an interesting study from a contemporary point of view, within a careful reconstruction of Descartes' project in B. Williams' *Descartes* (Stanford 1978). E. Curley's *Descartes Against the Skeptics* (Oxford 1978) is also important. In the 1970s the most significant contribution from French scholars was J. M. Beyssade's *La philosophie première de Descartes: le temps et la cohérence de la métaphysique* (Paris 1979). A compilation of some of Beyssade's papers can be found in *Études sur Descartes* (Paris: Seuil, 2001) and in *Descartes ai fil de 'ordre* (Paris: PUF, 2001). A concise exposition of metaphysics and, in general, Descartes' philosophy can be found in G. Rodis-Lewis, *L'oeuvre de Descartes* (Paris 1971).

The following decade was dominated by the several contributions treating Descartes' metaphysics by J. L. Marion, with clear traces of Heidegger's influence in his interpretation of metaphysics. Among them are *Sur la théologie blanche de*

Descartes (Paris 1981) and *Sur le prisme métaphysique de Descartes* (Paris 1986). Marion's brief works of Descartes, concentrating on aspects of Cartesian metaphysics, were gathered in two collections: *Questions cartésiennes* (Paris 1991) and *Questions cartésiennes, II* (Paris 1996).

In German academia the most significant monographs come to us from W. Röd: *Descartes Erste Philosophie* (Bonn 1971) and *Descartes. Die Genese des cartesianischen Rationalismus* (Munich 1982).

There are many important brief and concise contributions scattered about, but an excellent selection of Cartesian literature containing a vast collection of these papers is now available in *Descartes: Critical Assesments,* edited by G J. D. Moyal (London-New York 1991).

Other important works on the metaphysical thought of Descartes are found in W. Doney's (ed.) *Descartes: A Collection of Critical Essays* (New York 1967); B. Magnus and J. B. Wilbur, eds. *Cartesian Essays: A Collection of Critical Studies* (The Hague 1969); R. Butler, ed. *Cartesian Studies* (Oxford 1972); M. Hooker, ed. *Descartes: Critical and Interpretive Essays* (Baltimore-London 1978); A. Rorty Oksenberg, ed. *Essays on Descartes' Meditations* (Berkeley-Los Angeles-London 1986); W. Doney, ed. *Eternal Truths and the Cartesian Circle: A Collection of Studies* (New York-London 1987); G. Rodis-Lewis, ed. *Méthode et Métaphysique chez Descartes* (New York-London 1987); J. Cottingham, ed. *The Cambridge Companion to Descartes* (Cambridge, 1992); V. Chappell, ed. *Descartes' Meditations: Critical Essays* (Lanham, 1997); S. Gaukroger, ed. *The Blackwell Guide to Descartes' Meditations* (London, 2003); J. Broughton, J. Carriero, eds. *A Companion to Descartes* (Oxford, 2008).

There transpired a conference dedicated to the study of the relationship between the *Meditations* and the *Objections and Replies* appropriately entitled *Descartes: Objecter et répondre* which took place at the Sorbonne, October 1992. The proceedings were published under the editorial command of J. M. Beyssade and J. L. Marion (Paris 1994).

S. Di Bella's *Meditazioni metafisiche. Introduzione alla lettura* (Rome: NIS, 1997) is an accurate presentation of the *Meditations*. For a careful reading of the First Meditation and of the critical literature on the subject see D. Kambouchner, *Les Méditations métaphysiques de Descartes. Introduction générale. Première Méditation* (Paris, 2005). See also, J. Carriero, *Between Two Worlds: A Reading of Descartes'* Meditations (Princeton, 2008). For an account of the metaphysical foundation of physics see D. Garber, *Descartes' Metaphysical Physics* (Chicago, 1992). For the connections between Descartes' metaphysics and Scholastic thought, see E. Gilson, *Index scholastico-cartésien* (Paris, 1913 and 1979); R. Ariew, *Descartes and the Last Scholastics* (Ithaca-London, 1998); J. Secada, *Cartesian Metaphysics* (Cambridge, 2000); E. Scribano, *Angeli e beati. Modeli di conoscenza da Tommaso a Spinoza* (Rome-Bari, 2006). With regard to references to St. Augustine in Descartes' works, see Z. Janowski, *Augustinian-Cartesian Index. Texts and Commentary* (South Bend, Indiana, 2004).

* * * * *

The reader will find listed below further categories of interest regarding major themes of the *Meditations of First Philosophy*, as they appear in this reading guide as well as relevant contemporary scholarship. The reader must note that these arguments are nevertheless, in one way or another, contained in the monographs aforementioned.

On the History of the Text

H. Gouhier. "Pour une histoire des *Méditations* métaphysiques," in *Revue des Sciences humaines* 1951: 5–29; and *Etudes d'histoire de la philosophie française* (Hildesheim-New York, 1976), 7–31.

G. Crapulli. "La rédaction et les projets d'édition des *Meditationes de prima philosophia* de Descartes," in *Les études philosophiques* (1976): 425–441; (1977): 369–370.

G. Crapulli. "La prima edizione delle *Meditationes de prima philosophia* di Descartes e il suo esemplare ideale," in *Studia cartesiana* I(1979):37–90.

G. Crapulli. "La seconda edizione delle *Meditationes de prima philosophia* di Descartes (1642) nei suoi rapporti con la prima (1641)," in *Atti del I Seminario internazionale sulla trasmissione dei testi a stampa nel periodo moderno: Rome, June 23–25, 1983*, edited by G. Crapulli (Rome, 1985), 77–112).

On Doubt

R. H. Popkin. *The History of Skepticism From Erasmus to Descartes* (Assen, 1960), 174–217.

N. Malcolm. "Dreaming and Skepticism," in *The Philosophical Review* 65(1965): 14–37.

J. M. Beyssade. "Mais quoi, ce sont des fous. Sur un passage controversé de la Première Méditation," in *Revue de Métaphysique et de Morale* 78(1973): 273–94.

P. A. Schouls. "The Extent of Doubt in Descartes' Meditations," in *Canadian Journal of Philosophy* 3(1973): 51–58.

T. Gregory. "Dio ingannatore e genio maligno. Nota in margine alle *Meditationes* di Descartes," in *Giornale critico della filosofia italiana* 53(1974): 477–516.

W. Röd. "L'argument de rêve dans la doctrine cartésienne de l'expérience," in *Les Etudes philosophiques* (1976): 461–73.

W. H. O'Briant. "Doubting the Truths of Mathematics in Descartes' Meditations," in *Southern Journal of Philosophy* 15(1977): 527–35.

D. Sievert. "Does Descartes Doubt Everything?" in *The New Scholasticism* 53(1979): 107–17.

M. A. Olson. "Descartes' First Meditation: Mathematics and the Laws of Logic," in *Journal of the History of Philosophy* 26(1988): 407–437.

J. P. Cavaillé. "Les sens trompeurs. Usage cartésien d'un motif sceptique," in *Revue Philosophique* 116(1991): 3–31.

E. Scribano. "L'inganno divino nelle *Meditazioni* di Descartes," in *Rivista di filosofia* 90(1990): 219–251.

G. Paganini. *Skepsis. Le débat des modernes sur le scepticisme* (Paris, 2008), see chapter V.

On the Cogito

H. Scholz. "Über das *Cogito ergo sum*," in *Kant-Studien* 36(1931):126–47.

G. Dreyfus. "Discussion sur le 'cogito' et l'axiome 'pour penser, il faut être,'" in *Revue Internationale de Philosophie* 19(1952): 117–25.

J. Hintikka. "Cogito Ergo Sum Inference or Performance?" in *The Philosophical Review* 71(1962): 3–32.

H. Frankfurt. "Descartes: Discussion of His Existence in the Second Meditation," in *The Philosophical Review* 75 (1966): 329–56.

J. B. Wilbur. "The Cogito, an Ambiguous Performance," in *Cartesian Essays,* J. B. Wilbur, B. Magnus, eds.

F. Feldman. "On the Performatory Interpretation of the Cogito," in *The Philosophical Review* 82(1973): 345–63.

W. Röd. "Einige Überlegungen zur Debatte über das 'Cogito ergo sum' in der Philosophie des 20. Jahrhunderts," in *Studia Cartesiana* I (1979):129–44.

On Ideas and Thought

A.Gewirth. "A Clearness and Distinction in Descartes," in *Philosophy* 18(1943):17–36.

T. J. Cronin. *Objective Being in Descartes and Suarez* (Rome, 1966).

N. J. Wells. "Objective Being: Descartes and His Sources," in *The Modern Schoolman* 45(1967–1968): 49–61.

J. C. Doig. "Suarez, Descartes, and the Objective Reality of Ideas," in *The New Scholasticism* 51(1977): 350–371.

E. J. Kearns. *Ideas in Seventeenth-century France* (Manchester, 1979).

M. J. Costa. "What Cartesian Ideas are Not," in *Journal of the History of Philosophy* 21(1983): 537–49.

N. J. Wells. "Material Falsity in Descartes, Arnauld, and Suarez," in *Journal of the History of Philosophy* 22(1984): 25–50.

F. Van de Pitte. "Descartes' Innate Ideas," in *Kant-Studien* 76(1985): 362–84.

D. Radner. "Thought and Consciousness in Descartes," in *Journal of the History of Philosophy* 26(1988): 439–52.

N. J. Wells. "Objective Reality of Ideas in Descartes, Caterus, and Suarez," in *Journal of the History of Philosophy* 28(1990): 33–61.

W. Edelberg. "The Fifth Meditation," in *The Philosophical Review* 99(1990): 493–533.

N. J. Wells. "Descartes: Ideas and His Sources," in *American Catholic Philosophical Quarterly* 67(1993): 523–535.

E. Scribano. "Descartes et les fausses idés," in *Archives de Philosophie* 64(2001): 259–278.

S. Landucci. *La mente in Cartesio* (Milan, 2002).

L. Alanen. *Descartes' Concept of the Mind* (Cambridge, Massachusetts, 2003).

C. Wee. *Material Falsity and Error in Descartes'* Meditations (London-New York, 2006).

D. Clemson. *Descartes; Theory of Ideas* (London-New York, 2007).

E. Angelini. *Le idee e le cose. La teoria della percezione de Descartes* (Pisa, 2007).

D. J. Brown. *Descartes on Innate Ideas* (London-New York, 2009).

On Ideas and the Eternal Truths

E. Boutroux. *De veritatibus aeternis apud Cartesium* (Paris, 1874).

E. Gilson. *La liberté chez Descartes et la théologie* (Paris, 1913).

É. Bréhier. "La création des vérités éternelles dans le système de Descartes," in *Revue philosophique* (1937).

H. G. Frankfurt. "Descartes on the Creation of Eternal Truths," in *The Philosophical Review* I (1977): 36–57.

G. Brown. "Vera Entia: The Nature of Mathematical Objects in Descartes," in *Journal of the History of Philosophy* 18(1980): 23–37.

N. J. Wells. "Descartes' Uncreated Eternal Truths," in *The New Scholasticism* (1982): 185–99.

S. Landucci. "La creazione delle verità eterne," in *La teodicea nell'età cartesiana* (Napoli, 1986), 127–193.

W. Doney, ed. *Eternal Truths and the Cartesian Circle* (New York, 1987).

T. M. Schmaltz. "Platonism and Descartes' View of Immutable Essences," in *Archiv für Geschichte der Philosophie* 73(1991): 129–70.

L. Nolan. "The Ontological Status of Cartesian Natures," in *Pacific Philosophical Quarterly* 78(1997).

L. Nolan. "Descartes' Theory of Universals," in *Philosophical Studies* 89(1998): 161–180.

J. L. Marion. *Sur la théologie blanche de Descartes,* op. cit.

On God and Proofs of God's Existence

A. Koyré. *Essai sur l'idé de Dieu et les preuves de son existence chez Descartes* (Paris, 1922).

P. Lachièze-Rey. *Les origines cartésiennes de Dieu de Spinoza* (Paris, 1950).

D. Henrich. *Der ontologische Gottesbeweis* (Tübingen, 1967).

W. L. Rowe. "Descartes' Cosmological Argument," in *The Monist* 54(1970): 427–459.

R. Delahunty. "Descartes' Cosmological Argument," in *The Philosophical Quarterly* 30(1980): 34–46.

J. L. Friedman. "Necessity and the Ontological Argument," in *Erkenntnis* 15(1980): 301–331.

W. Doney. "L'argument de Descartes à partir de la toute-puissance," in *Recherches sur le XVII siècle* 7(1984): 59–68.

J. D. Moyal. "La preuve ontologique dans l'ordre des raisons," in *Revue de Métaphysique et de Morale* 93(1988): 246–251.

J. L. Marion. "L'argument relève-t-il de l'ontologie?" in *L'argomento ontologico*. M. M. Olivetti, ed. Also in, *Archivio di filosofia* 58(1990): 43–69.

J. M. Beyssade. "The Idea of God and the Proofs of His Existence," in *Descartes,* J. Cottingham, ed. (Cambridge, 1992), 174–99.

Scribano, E. *L'esistenza di Dio. Storia della prova ontologica da Descartes a Kant* (Rome-Bari, 1994).

A. Goudriaan. *Philosophiche Gotteserkenntnis bei Suarez und Descartes* (Leiden-Boston-Koln, 1999).

L. Devillairs. *Descartes et la connaissance de Dieu* (Paris, 2004).

I. Agostini. *L'idea di Dio in Descartes* (Milan, 2010).

L. Nolan. "Descartes' Ontological Argument," in *The Stanford Encyclopedia of Philosophy (2001–2011)*.

On the Theory of Judgment and Error

J. L. Evans. "Error and the Will," in *Philosophy* 38 (1963): 136–48.

H. Caton. "Will and Reason in Descartes' Theory of Error," in *The Journal of Philosophy* 72 (1975): 87–104.

F. Van De Pitte. "Intuition and Judgment in Descartes' Theory of Truth," in *Journal of the History of Philosophy* 26 (1988): 453–70.

On Freedom and the Will

E. Gilson. *La liberté chez Descartes et la théologie* (Paris, 1913).

J. Laporte. "La liberté selon Descartes," in *Revue de métaphysique et de morale* (1937): 101–64. Also in *Etudes d'histoire de la philosophie au XVII siècle* (Paris 1951), 37–87.

A. Kenny. "Descartes on the Will," in *Cartesian Studies*, R. J. Butler, ed. See 2–31.

G. Canziani. *Filosofia e scienza nella morale di Descartes* (Florence, 1980), 173–212.

N. Grimaldi. *Six Etudes sur la volonté et la liberté chez Descartes* (Paris, 1988).

M. Beyssade. "Descartes' Doctrine of Freedom: Differences Between the French and Latin Texts of the Fourth Meditation," in *Reason, Will, and Sensation. Studies in Descartes' Metaphysics*. J. Cottingham, ed. (Oxford, 1994), 191–206.

H. Bouchilloux. *La question de la liberté chez Descartes* (Paris, 2003).

On Cartesian Theodicy

S. Landucci. *La teodicea nell'età cartesiana* (Naples, 1986).

Z. Janowski. *Cartesian Theodicy: Descartes' Quest For Certitude* (Dordrecht-Boston-London, 2000).

On the Mind and the Body

N. Malcolm. *Problems of Mind: Descartes to Wittgenstein* (New York, 1971), see chapter one, 1–59.

D. Radner. "Descartes' Notion of the Union of Mind and Body," in *Journal of the History of Philosophy* 9(1971): 159–70.

R. A. Watson. "What Moves the Mind: An Excursion in Cartesian Dualism," in *American Philosophical Quarterly* 19(1982): 73–81.

J. L. Vieillard-Baron, ed. *Autor de Descartes. Le dualsime de l'âme et du corps* (Paris, 1991).

G. F. Cantelli. *La parola come similitudine dell'uomo. Una interpretazione del rapporto mente-corpo in Cartesio* (Naples, 1992).

K.J. Morris. *Descartes' Dualism* (London-New York, 1995).

C.Kolesnik-Antoine. *L'homme cartésien* (Rennes, 2009).

On the Cartesian Circle

R.D. Hughes, "Le 'cercle' des Méditations: un état des recherches récentes," in *Archives de philosophie*, 1978, 1–12.

J. Etchemendy. "The Cartesian Circle: Circulus ex tempore," in *Studia Cartesiana* 2(1981): 5–42.

W. Doney, ed. *Eternal Truths and the Cartesian Circle. A Collection of Studies* (New York-London 1987).

Index of Names